"While the institutional church persisted in a narrative of exclusion, LGBT+ Christians gave Christian communities the quiet, persistent grace of their presence, their gifts, and their love. Now they add grace to grace by sharing the intimacy, vulnerability, and power of their stories, narratives of God's embrace. Here we have an opportunity to listen and hear anew God's resounding 'yes' to these siblings who have too often been told 'no' by human voices. In hearing, we have a fresh occasion to add our amen to God's declarations of love."

—**J. R. Daniel Kirk**
Pastoral Director, Newbigin House of Studies

"*Our Witness* is a must read! My congratulations to Brandan Robertson for bringing together a beautiful collection of stories . . . some heart breaking . . . some heartwarming . . . but all showing our need and God's desire for a fully inclusive church for all God's children. Because I believe strongly that stories can change hearts and minds I see God's light shining brightly through the lives of each and every one of these brave people. People who so willingly and beautifully articulate and share their stories to help foster hope, peace and life for so many others."

—**Jane Clementi**
Co-Founder, The Tyler Clementi Foundation

"This compilation of LGBT Christian stories clearly shows how loving, faithful people have been excluded by bad theologians who continue to put forth bad theology. It shows the alarming effects: depression and even suicide. Brandon has taken all his and others pain and puts forward a positive theology. And perhaps most importantly, he states and explains why 'homosexuality is not a sin' . . . and that is critical to save vulnerable lives, be true to the spirit of Christian values and make our world a better place . . . for everyone!"

—**Mitchell Gold**
Co-Founder, Mitchell Gold + Bob Williams

"*Our Witness* is a breath-taking, essential look at faithful Christians working to be the body of Christ even as Christians marginalize and reject them. I was moved to tears even as I was filled with hope—these folks represent the best of our faith."

—**Mike McHargue**
host of *The Liturgists Podcast* and author of *Finding God in the Waves*

"The stories of witness which Christians have told, but which have not been heard, typify much of Christian history. The sad but powerful words of witness in this book are a sign of the gospel which allows LGBT+ voices to be heard. They offer an urgent message which needs to be heeded by Christians in this and every generation."

—**Christopher Rowland**
Professor of the Exegesis of Holy Scripture Emeritus, University of Oxford

"Brandan's new book, *Our Witness*, continues his tradition of moving the Church forward in its acceptance of LGBTQ individuals and being the inclusive institution that it is meant to be. Brandan challenges us readers to listen to voices that we may never have heard before. Their stories are extremely powerful and have the ability to shift people's paradigms. I pray that many church leaders will read its pages and be transformed. It would benefit the Church and the world."

—**David W. Key, Sr.**
National Board Chair, Association of Welcoming and Affirming Baptists

"This is a tremendous collection of deeply moving stories. Some of them are heart-rending, some wonderfully positive, some both. I hope before long such a book will be neither needed nor possible."

—**Professor Michael J Reiss**
UCL Institute of Education, University College London

"This book richly deserves to be read by LGBT Christians, for the healing it will help to bring—and by non-LGBT Christians, who will surely learn from it about some important truths about LGBT lives."

—**Terry Weldon**
Deputy Chair, Quest Gay Catholics

"In *Nomad: A spirituality for travelling light* Brandan Robertson, a young man with a deep faith, engaging life experience, and mature spiritual insights, shared with the world the story of his own journey. In editing this book—*Our Witness*—he enables and empowers others to tell their own profoundly moving and challenging stories in a way that invites us all to hear and to engage with them. Attentive listening, together with active and selfless hearing, are essential qualities to bring to bear on dialogue between Christians, and, indeed, within a divided world."

—**Paul Colton**
Bishop of Cork, Ireland

"This book is exactly what the modern church needs! Brandan Robertson has done an amazing job of assembling and connecting us to the lives of our brothers and sisters, who have journeyed and wrestled with the hard and complicated questions of human sexuality. No matter where you stand on queer theology, this is a must read . . . for it is the stories of the human condition, that gives us the ability to see 'the other' with the eyes of Christ."

—**Richard McCullen**
Lead Visionary Missiongathering Movement, Disciples of Christ

"These faith-stories of people with diverse sexualities and gender identities show all the people of God what riches of faithful discipleship and spirituality can be found at the heart of all our varied Christian communities."

—**Martin Pendergast**
LGBT Catholics Westminster Pastoral Council

OUR WITNESS

OUR WITNESS

The Unheard Stories of LGBT+ Christians

EDITED BY
BRANDAN ROBERTSON

FOREWORD BY
LISBETH M. MELÉNDEZ RIVERA

AFTERWORD BY
JOSEPH TOLTON

CASCADE *Books* · Eugene, Oregon

OUR WITNESS
The Unheard Stories of LGBT+ Christians

Copyright © 2018 Wipf and Stock Publishers. All rights reserved. Except for brief quotations in critical publications or reviews, no part of this book may be reproduced in any manner without prior written permission from the publisher. Write: Permissions, Wipf and Stock Publishers, 199 W. 8th Ave., Suite 3, Eugene, OR 97401.

Cascade Books
An Imprint of Wipf and Stock Publishers
199 W. 8th Ave., Suite 3
Eugene, OR 97401

www.wipfandstock.com

PAPERBACK ISBN: 978-1-5326-1067-7
HARDCOVER ISBN: 978-1-5326-1069-1
EBOOK ISBN: 978-1-5326-1068-4

Cataloging-in-Publication data:

Names: Robertson, Brandan, editor. | Melendez Rivera, Lisbeth M., foreword. | Tolton, Joseph, afterword.

Title: Our witness : the unheard stories of LGBT+ Christians / edited by Brandan Robertson; foreword by Lisbeth M. Melendez Rivera; afterword by Joseph Tolton.

Description: Eugene, OR : Cascade Books, 2018 | Includes bibliographical references.

Identifiers: ISBN 978-1-5326-1067-7 (paperback) | ISBN 978-1-5326-1069-1 (hardcover) | ISBN 978-1-5326-1068-4 (ebook)

Subjects: LCSH: Homosexuality—Religious aspects—Christianity. | Gays—Religious life—Christianity. | Christian gays.

Classification: LCC BR115.H6 O88 2018 (print) | LCC BR115.H6 (ebook)

03/23/18

Contents

Foreword

Lisbeth M. Meléndez Rivera

When we speak we like to be heard, listened to, not judged, but simply listened to. So many of us are unheard, ignored by those who pretend to love us, and so many times it's done in the name of God.

Love is the language of acceptance, the embrace of the different, the listening of the unheard. For many Christians this is a language denied. Yet Jesus teaches us the importance of listening—listening to God in prayer, listening to one another in living—and when listening to suspend judgment, for judgment is not the language of love. When you listen you can hear God's love and it must not fall on unhearing ears.

So many of us walk this planet seeking the dignity afforded to those who are heard, those whose words elevate the discourse and expand the understanding of our faith. We are called to ensure all of us are not just heard but listened to.

The stories of LGBTQ people of faith can be found in everyday conversations. They demonstrate the glory of a Creator who sees beauty in all they create and all they continue to perfect.

As we work to make sure the voices of all children of God are heard, I am proud we will have these stories to add to our world. In these pages you will read the stories of those who have gone unheard, whose lives have been made invisible by a Christianity reduced to the judgment of man not the love of God. In collecting these moments, these lives, these narratives, Brandan Robertson does what many of us yearn for: gives Christians a canvas in which they get to paint in words the pains and the joys of survival. Yes, these will be painful to read in many cases, but push through, honor the resilience of those who dare show us what we can do to one another when we choose to not see, to not hear the lament and the hurt of those who have been denied the love of God. What you will learn at the end is that regardless of what we do to one another, many of us will not just survive but thrive. You will see our wounds and experience healing. At the very least you will witness and honor our journeys.

Come join me in learning, listening, and honoring those brave enough to show us their pain and a way to love and be embraced by love. Make their telling heard.

Lisbeth Meléndez Rivera is the Human Rights Campaigns Director of Latino and Catholic Initiatives. Lisbeth also worked as the National Co-ordinator for the *A la Familia* project, training and empowering Latinos/as throughout country regarding LGBTQ issues. Lisbeth envisioned and directed *Before God: We Are All Family*, a powerful short documentary that has been shared with Latino/a communities across the country.

Acknowledgments

Editing a book like this is no small feat. I have been so humbled and honored by the whole process. The courage, vulnerability, and hope shared in the over 100 essays submitted from every corner of the globe has reignited my passion and belief that God is really up to something in and through LGBT+ people of faith. To the team at Wipf and Stock/Cascade for believing in this project, thank you!

To the amazing team that helped me wade through the first rounds of edits on the essays in this book: Sheri Rosenthal, Jessica Honeycutt, Brody Levesque, Michael Wright, Rhiannon Hall, and Ruairidh MacRae, *thank you* so much for your help. This project could not have been the amazing collection of stories that it is if it wasn't for your skillful proofreading and suggestions. To Pastor Ray Shawn McKinnon who financially supported the process of editing this collection and whose vibrancy always inspires me—thank you!

To my thesis advisor at Iliff School of Theology, Dr. Katherine Turpin, for your invaluable insights that made my thesis and the theological foundation for this book so much stronger.

To the LGBT+ pioneers that have served as friends, mentors, and guides to me along my own journey of reconciling my faith and sexuality: Bishop Gene Robinson, Macky Alston, Bishop Karen Olivteo, Rev. Jim Mitulski, Rich Tafel, Vicky Beeching, John McConnell, Jonathan Rauch, Sharon Groves, Paula Williams. Your encouragement and witness continues to be the fuel that keeps me doing this work. Thank you!

To the innumerable great cloud of LGBT+ witnesses who have gone before us, paving the way for the work of the Spirit in our day, may you be honored by our stories and our gratitude for the path that you have paved to make our journey easier.

To all of the LGBT+ people whose lives have ended far too early as a result of the toxic teachings and practices on noninclusion, may this book serve as a solemn remembrance of your lives and be one more step toward complete abolishing of toxic, anti-LGBT+ theology in the church.

To all of the LGBT+ people of faith who are still standing in the closet. May these stories be a reminder that *you are not alone* and that your are wildly loved, just as you are.

To our expansive, diverse, and creative God, who calls us out of the shadows and into the light of our Truest Selves, may you be glorified and honored by this work, and may you use these stories to spread the Good News of your liberation and inclusion far and wide for ages to come.

Introduction

Not Untold, but Unheard

Brandan Robertson

The stories of LGBT+ Christians are not *untold*, but they are often *unheard*. Throughout the history of Christianity, LGBT+ people have played an integral role in their communities of faith, whether or not they were able to be open about their sexuality or gender identity. We have produced good fruit and often been some of the brightest lights for the Gospel of Christ in the world. But so often when we are brave enough to speak about our sexuality or gender identity, our light is forced under a bushel and we are cast out from the communities that we have loved and served. After we are expelled for embracing our God-given identity, we are silenced. Our voices are drowned out by the sound of dogmatic preaching about being "unnatural," "abominations," or "threats to family values." Our voices are ignored by church leaders who sit high in their ivory towers, refusing to acknowledge the legitimacy of our lives and our faith for fear that doing so would threaten their own position of privilege. Our voices are even sometimes silenced by our families whose cold obedience to church teachings leads them to force us into programs to change our identity or push us out of their lives until we "repent" for being who we are.

But in the midst of all of this abuse and injustice, we keep speaking. In every city, in every denomination, in every church, there are LGBT+ Christians who refuse to be silenced; who heed the call of Christ to proclaim the truth and shine their light without fear of persecution or rejection; who continue to fight for their place at the table of God's grace; or who decide to make their own tables in their own faith communities that embrace the truly radical message of God's unconditional love and acceptance of all. When all of the church tells us to sit down and be silent, we continue to speak. We continue to embrace the love of God. We continue to follow the radically subversive way of Jesus. And as we do, we're bringing the queer masses with us.

In 2015, the Pew Research Institute released a poll that showed while every major demographic of Christians was on decline, one of the only areas where there was a steady uptick in identification as "Christian" was among the LGBT+ community.[1] Around the world, LGBT+ Christian organizations and churches are popping up, drawing thousands upon thousands of LGBT+ people of faith and their allies together to worship, learn, and dream about how they can be more faithful disciples of Christ. And yet, a majority of Christians around the world *don't know that this is happening.* Or worse, they *deny* that this is happening because this evidence of the Holy Spirit's work among open and proud LGBT+ people directly contradicts their theological paradigm. But when your theology and your reality contradict, it may be time to rethink your theology.

The Spirit of God is moving among sexual and gender minorities on every continent around the world. Openly LGBT+ people are being raised to the highest levels of leadership in churches, organizations, and denominations. And while those seeking to resist the evidence of the Holy Spirit's work among these devoted followers of Jesus shout loudly from their pulpits and publishing houses, it seems to me that the voices of LGBT+ Christians are only getting louder and harder to ignore. Whether worship leaders, pastors, celebrities, bloggers, activists, or laypeople, LGBT+ Christians are boldly and bravely reclaiming our rightful place in the Body of Christ. We have a story to tell, a message to share, a Gospel to proclaim, and the church would be wise to quiet their own voice of resistance and listen to what the Spirit of God might be speaking to them through us.

My own journey of faith and sexuality has been a rough one. I first realized that I was bisexual when I was a pre-teen. I remember sitting in the back of my church, realizing that I had an uncontrollable sense of attraction to another young man a few pews in from of me. I ran out of the sanctuary to the bathroom to ask God to forgive me for this "destructive" attraction,

---

1. "America's Changing Religious Landscape," Pew Research Center, May 12, 2015, http://www.pewforum.org/2015/05/12/americas-changing-religious-landscape/.

seeking to be healed. As years went on, my commitment to Christ grew stronger, but my sexual orientation never seemed to change. When I was finally in Bible college, studying to be a pastor, I began confessing my "struggle" to friends on my floor during our "accountability" meetings and quickly found that *many* of the men studying at my school *also* struggled with "same-sex attraction." All of us had strong callings to ministry and had flourishing relationships with God, but lived in constant terror that this fundamental part of our identity would somehow render us damaged at best, damned at worst.

The realization of how fearful we all were about our sexuality led me on a journey of deep biblical study and prayer. I visited churches, met with theologians, read books, and began to realize that *maybe* the Bible *wasn't* quite as clear in its condemnation of LGBT+ people as I once thought. *Maybe* the openly LGBT+ Christians I had encountered truly *did* have a relationship with God. *Maybe* God didn't make a mistake in his creation of LGBT+ people. As I began to come to these realizations, I also began a conversion therapy program as a last ditch effort to see if God truly desired to heal me of being bisexual. After a year of trying to be healed of my sexuality and of wrestling with God, I finally came to a sense of peace in my heart about who I was. I felt the Spirit reassuring me that I had nothing to fear. At the same time, I knew I couldn't speak about this peace and assurance to anyone in my college or my church because it would lead to certain expulsion. So I remained in hiding.

As soon as I graduated from Bible college, I moved to Washington, DC, and decided that I needed to work hard to advocate on behalf of LGBT+ people in the church. I wasn't "out" publicly yet, but I felt the Spirit tugging at my heart, telling me that the next step in my vocation was to do work that would be incredibly costly, but essential. I stepped into the role of national spokesperson for a new organization called Evangelicals for Marriage Equality, founded by two straight evangelical men from opposite sides of the political spectrum, but who both felt convicted that Evangelical Christians should not be seeking to prevent LGBT+ people from having equal rights in our society. We launched our organization with an op-ed in *TIME Magazine*, where I wrote about my own sense of conviction about how my fellow Christians were doing great damage to the cause of Christ in our world by seeking to marginalize and prevent LGBT+ people from having equal rights under the law. Within twenty-four hours, leaders from the Southern Baptist Convention responded to our article with their own op-ed in *TIME,* as well as on national radio, podcasts, and various other blogs and articles. Overnight, I went from being a "faithful Christian" in the eyes of many, to a deceived heretic—and they didn't even know that I identified as LGBT+ yet.

Over the next six months, I would be invited to participate in conversations with major evangelical leaders on radio and in front of live audiences, and every time I was publicly shamed for my position and told that I was leading many into destruction. This culminated in February of 2015, when I turned in the manuscript of my first book, *Nomad*, to my Christian publisher and was abruptly told that unless I signed a statement condemning same-sex relationships as contrary to God's created plan, then they could not publish my book. When I saw this email, I knew that I could no longer hide the truth of what I believed and where I stood in regards to my own sexuality. I wrote back to my publisher and let them know that I wouldn't sign their statement, and soon after was told that my book contract had been canceled. When news of this story reached a reporter at *TIME Magazine*, she told me that she wanted to write a story about this loss, but that she wanted to tell the *full* story, including the truth about my sexuality. At this point, I knew it was time. I knew that if I remained closeted and hiding in fear, I would be doing more harm than good for myself and for the LGBT+ people that were being affected by the public work I was engaged in. I agreed to let the reporter write a story, under the condition that I be given a few weeks to come out to my friends and family. She agreed, and we moved forward with the story.

Just a few days after talking with the reporter, I was sitting in a room playing a game with some friends and my phone began to vibrate uncontrollably. Message after message began to pour in by the dozens. I had no clue what was going on. I opened my text-messaging app and saw the first one was from the reporter at *TIME*—"I'm so sorry! My editors published the piece early by mistake!" her message read. I felt my heart skip a beat, as I scrolled over to Facebook to find myself tagged in a headline that said "Young Evangelical Leader Loses Book Deal After Coming Out." [2] The only problem with the headline was that I *hadn't* come out to most of my friends or family yet, and the flurry of messages I received were from people in my life responding, both with affirmation and strong condemnation, to the

2. See the article here: Elizabeth Dias, "Young Evangelical Leader Loses Book Deal After Coming Out," *TIME*, February 21, 2015, http://time.com/3716350/brandan-roberston-destiny-image/.

revelation of my true sexual identity. The next few days are now a blur to me, but they were filled with some of the warmest embraces and coldest condemnations from various mentors and friends in my life. My family reacted surprisingly well, which was a relief. But some of my closest mentors filled my inbox with messages like:

> I wonder [if] you tell the people how dishonest, cunning and manipulative you are. I wonder whether you tell them about your addictions and compulsions. I wonder whether you tell them about how actively you cultivate a sin life while being so inactive towards righteousness and how damningly lazy you are? Do you tell them how disinterested you are in the Word? So where exactly do the bridges you allegedly build lead? Certainly you are a leader, Brandan. It is safe to say that in the current trajectory of your life you will usher many into a hellish existence. And when you need the blood of Christ to wash away your sins, where will you turn, now that you have renounced His redeeming and transforming work so thoroughly? I know you like to be coddled. True words feel so harsh to you. (This, of course, keeps the door to your personal prison locked.) Nevertheless, only one word makes sense to speak: Repent.[3]

I had experienced rejection for my support of marriage equality before, but now that I was publicly identified as LGBT+, the words of condemnation I received were harsher and more cutting than ever. For the first time, I really experienced the harm and deep wounds that so many of my LGBT+ friends have told me about. I knew this would some day be a reality I faced, but I never really counted the cost. Now I was being personally attacked by those who once loved me, I was told that my future in pastoral ministry within my evangelical context would never be a reality, and I became a scapegoat for so many non-affirming Christians to throw all sorts of accusations upon.

When all of this was happening, I entered into a period of severe sorrow. But it wasn't sorrow for myself or my future—I believed that I would make it through this and was relentlessly committed to pursuing my calling regardless of what my opponents said. My grief instead was for the church. A community of people who have committed their lives to follow the life and teachings of Jesus, who so quickly had turned to cast stones at me and so many other LGBT+ people simply because they disagreed with us over

---

3. This is a quote from an actual email I received from an actual former mentor of mine. Some details of the quote have been omitted or changed for privacy reasons.

the interpretation of six verses in the Bible. Until I experienced the full force of rejection and condemnation of many in the church, I never truly understood just how *un-Christlike* the churches posture toward LGBT+ people really was. On dozens of important theological and social issues, Christians have agreed to remain in unity in the midst of their disagreements. But on this one issue—one that effects so many people at the most intimate levels of their being—the church has chosen a posture of full-on attack and rejection, and in doing so, has isolated and harmed so many beautiful, talented, faithful followers of Christ.

My sorrow over the church's response to LGBT+ people has continued to this day, but it has now largely been overshadowed by a profound, subversive hope. Over the past five years, I have met *thousands* of LGBT+ Christians around the world, and have witnessed the work of the Holy Spirit moving through them in the most profound ways. I have been blown away by how many major, global Christian leaders have reached out to tell me that they too have felt the Spirit of God nudging them to step forward and embrace LGBT+ people as faithful members of Christ's church. I have watched as societies around the world have stepped closer and closer to affirming and embracing LGBT+ people as equal and essential parts of their communities. And I have seen *true revival* breaking forth in the midst of LGBT+ Christian communities. So while I am continually grieved as I watch my brave LGBT+ siblings step out of the darkness and into the light of who God made them to be while being subsequently abused by Christians, I am also profoundly confident that this movement we are a part of is a movement of the Holy Spirit of God, and that nothing and no one will be able to stop this wild river of inclusion. The more that straight, non-affirming Christians witness the work of God in and through the lives and stories of LGBT+ people, the more I see hearts of stone soften, and the doors of churches open just a little wider to welcome LGBT+ people into our rightful place at the table of Grace.

And *that* is the inspiration and vision behind this book. Because I believe that God is doing a new thing through LGBT+ people, and I also believe that the only way for anyone to truly understand this movement of God is to hear the authentic, raw stories of LGBT+ Christians. Since the very beginning of our faith, Christians have been a people of *story* and of *testimony*. We have always known that when people hear our stories and experience life through our eyes, hearts and minds will change. And these brave siblings of mine have poured out their souls onto these pages, giving you a glimpse into their authentic struggles, pains, and triumphs. It is truly a *sacred privilege* that we get to be invited in to these lives together, and I hope that as you read these words, you feel humbled by the invitation that has been extended to you to enter into these lives and stories.

My hope for this book is twofold: First, that LGBT+ Christians and our allies will be able to hear the powerful witness contained in these stories and find strength, encouragement, and hope to continue to press on in our fight for inclusion. For my LGBT+ Christians siblings, I want you to know that you're not alone and that there *is* great reason to hope. For our allies, I hope that these stories add fuel to your fire, and that you will be moved to find ways to uplift the unheard voices of LGBT+ Christians in your communities.

Second, I challenge non-affirming Christians to read these stories in their entirety, without looking for points of disagreement or debate, but instead hearing the truth of the experiences of these LGBT+ Christians. As you read, I challenge you to be in prayer, opening yourself to whatever the Spirit of God might be saying to you through each life that is poured out in these pages. My goal isn't necessarily to convince you to change your mind, but for you to develop empathy and consider the great harm that has been done in the name of Jesus by those who hold your theological commitments. And after reading these stories, I hope that you will reach out to an LGBT+ person in your community and ask them to share with you their story as well, and that you might posture yourself in humility and repentance for the harm that has been done in the name of Christ by non-affirming Christians.

More than anything, my hope is that these words, these stories, these *lives* will bear witness to the power of the Love of God and the truly good news of the Gospel. I pray that as our collective light shines forth, many would see the good work that God is doing in and through us, and be moved to worship our expansive, diverse, and inclusive Creator.

PART 1

REJECTION

One of the most basic Christian tests for determining the truth of a doctrine or practice is based on the teaching of Jesus in the Gospel of Matthew, where he proclaims that one way his disciples can determine between true prophets and false prophets is "by their fruits."[1] This language of "fruits" appears numerous times throughout the New Testament[2] and plays off of the familiar first century agricultural imagery, which suggests that some crops yield "good fruits" (or a harvest that is luscious, edible, and profitable) compared to those crops that yield "bad fruits" (or a harvest that is diseased and scarce). Throughout the New Testament we are continually reminded that faithful followers of Jesus will bear "good fruits," or what the Apostle Paul calls "fruits of the spirit."[3] If one takes this call to discernment and examination of Christian teaching seriously, it naturally leads one to ask the question, "What is the result of a teaching on the lives of those who receive it?" If a teaching produces life and love, one could make the case that it bears good fruits, and therefore is a faithful and true teaching. Jesus' own life serves as our example of what good fruit looks like: standing up for the oppressed, welcoming the marginalized, and healing those who have been harmed by religious and political powers. But what if a teaching

1. Matt 7:16.
2. Matt 3:8–10; 7:16–20; 12:33; 21:43; Luke 6:43; John 15:5; Rom 7:4; Gal 5:22.
3. Gal 5:22.

produces death, mental harm, and fear? It seems that, following the logical pattern set forth in the Scriptures, we should condemn this teaching because of its "bad fruit" and it should be "cut down and thrown into the fire"[4] or hastily disregarded as "false."

Yet, when it comes to the teachings of the church about noninclusion, this biblical standard has been largely disregarded. Over the past decade, dozens of peer-reviewed studies have been done that have demonstrated a clear link to noninclusive religious teachings and practices to higher rates of depression and suicide in sexual and gender minorities. In 2012, the European Symposium of Suicide and Suicidal Behavior released a groundbreaking survey that suggested suicide rates among LGBT+ youth were significantly higher if the youth grew up in a religious context.[5] Similarly, dozens of studies from 2001 to 2015 have found links between religious affiliation and higher rates of depression and suicidality among LGBT+ adults.[6] A study published in 2014 by Jeremy Gibbs concluded:

> [Sexual Minority Youth] who mature in religious contexts, which facilitate identity conflict, are at higher odds for suicidal thoughts and suicide attempt compared to other SMY.[7]

Every year, new studies come out that suggest that noninclusive religious teachings result in higher rates of depression and suicidal ideation

4. Matt 7:19.

5. Jewish Press Staff, "Study: Highest Suicide Rates among Religious Homosexuals," *Jewish Press*, September 5, 2012, http://www.jewishpress.com/news/breaking-news/study-highest-rate-of-suicide-among-religious-homosexuals/2012/09/05/.

6. The following is a sampling of the multiple surveys and studies that I have examined for this article: R. R. Ganzevoort, M. Van der Laan, and E. Olsman, "Growing Up Gay and Religious: Conflict, Dialogue, and Religious Identity Strategies," *Mental Health, Religion, and Culture* 14 (2011) 209–22; Jeremy J. Gibbs and J. T. Goldbach, "Religious Conflict, Sexual Identity, and Suicidal Behaviors among LGBT Young Adults," *Archives of Suicide Research* 19 (2015) 472–88; J. T. Goldbach, E. F. Tanner-Smith, M. Bagwell, and S. Dunlap, "Minority Stress and Substance Use in Sexual Minority Adolescents: A Meta-Analysis," *Prevention Science* 15 (2014) 350–63; Arnold H. Grossman and Anthony R. D'Augelli, "Transgender Youth and Life-Threatening Behaviors," *Suicide and Life-Threatening Behavior* 37 (2007) 527–37; Víctor Figueroa and Fiona Tasker, "I Always Have the Idea of Sin in My Mind . . . ": Family of Origin, Religion, and Chilean Young Gay Men," *Journal of GLBT Family Studies* 10 (2014) 269–97.

7. Jeremy Goldbach and Jeremy Gibbs, "Growing Up Queer and Religious: A Quantitative Study Analyzing the Relationship between Religious Identity Conflict and Suicide in Sexual Minority Youth," Paper Presented at the 141st APHA Annual Meeting and Exposition, University of Southern California, 2013.

among LGBT+ youth and adults alike. These facts must be heeded by those in Christian leadership and should cause deep reflection on how their teaching and practices are complicit in these concerning trends.

While many conservative religious commentators have strongly pushed back against any suggestion that their theology has any actual effect on LGBT+ mental health and suicide rates, and in fact, will often use these statistics to suggest that it is not their teachings but rather the "gay lifestyle" that contributes to the mental distress of LGBT+ people,[8] these numbers and the experiences of LGBT+ people simply cannot be denied or ignored. Religious teachings that perpetuate the idea that sexual and gender minorities are somehow disordered, flawed, or sinful because of this piece of their identity has direct effects on the mental health of these individuals. Likewise, when straight congregants digest these teachings and are left to implement them practically in their own lives as they relate to LGBT+ people, it often translates to harsh rejection and condemnation. If the LGBT+ person is a youth, they may be forced into reparative therapy programs, a pseudo-psychological practice that has been condemned by every reputable[9] psychological association in the United States as dangerous to the health and wellbeing of LGBT+ people.[10] If a youth chooses to embrace their sexuality or gender identity, they are likely to be kicked out of their homes, driving up the rates of LGBT+ youth homelessness, which currently represents between 20–40 percent of all homeless youth.[11]

As one examines the evidence closely, the fruit of noninclusive religious teaching and practice is undeniably clear—it breeds death, rejection,

---

8. For examples, see Dr. Michael Brown's interview where he suggests LGBT+ rights activists use suicide victims as pawns to perpetuate the gay agenda: Brian Tashman, "Michael Brown: Gays Use Youth Suicide Victims as 'Pawns,'" *Right Wing Watch*, January 27, 2012, http://www.rightwingwatch.org/post/michael-brown-gays-use-youth-suicide-victims-as-pawns/.

9. By "reputable," I am referring to psychological associations that engage in peer reviewed studies and have been validated by the government as reliable sources of information, as opposed to the many smaller, religiously rooted psychological associations that are seen by the mainstream psychological community as engaging in a form of pseudo-psychology.

10. Human Rights Campaign, "Policy and Position Statements on Conversion Therapy," Human Rights Campaign, http://www.hrc.org/resources/policy-and-position-statements-on-conversion-therapy.

11. Nicholas Ray, "Lesbian, Gay, Bisexual, and Transgender Youth: An Epidemic of Homelessness," National Gay and Lesbian Task Force Policy Institute, 2006, http://www.thetaskforce.org/lgbt-youth-an-epidemic-of-homelessness/.

and severe psychological damage on sexual and gender minorities. It follows that these teachings should be "cast into the fire"[12] and religious theologians and practitioners of all stripes should be led back to their sacred texts and traditions to reassess the messages they are preaching, seeking to listen closely to the voice of the Spirit for a message that is truly good news and brings life to all people.

The following stories focus on the harm of rejection and the incredible damage done by nonaffirming theology and practice. Each of these stories goes into tremendous detail describing just how destructive noninclusion can be. The question that I invite you to consider as you read through each one of these accounts is this: could a true teaching of Christ *really* produce such harm? If the truth is supposed to produce *good fruit* and set people free, why then are an overwhelming majority of LGBT+ people so tremendously harmed by the church's teachings and practices in relation to their sexual orientation or gender identity? When our teaching and practice produces such pain and damage, perhaps it is time that we acknowledge they do not find their origin in God, and should be repented of and discarded for the good of our LGBT+ siblings in Christ.

12. Matt 7:19.

Celebrating Abomination

Katy-Anne Binstead

The blade plunged into me as I drew it across my skin causing an ugly red line of blood. I licked off the blood and continued with the practice making sure to punish myself severely. I needed to punish myself because my very existence was an abomination to God. I was a young woman who was equally attracted to both men and women and my religion taught that was sin against a holy God. So I would cut myself as atonement for my sin, forgetting that Jesus had already atoned for my sins (of which I had plenty, but being bisexual wasn't one of them).

The deed done, I hoped that God would forgive me for a while longer of being attracted to women as well as men, for looking at lesbian porn as well as regular porn, and for dating a hot woman. I had carefully hid this part of my life from my fundamentalist church because I would have been disciplined by the church had they found out and probably even thrown out. At the time, church was the only life that I knew. They were family to me. I had no other friends, just those at church as well as the young woman I was in a relationship with.

When it became obvious that I was still acting out on my sexuality, I sunk the blades in deeper, trying to kill myself, hoping that the ultimate act of death would atone for being such an abomination. At least I wouldn't be an abomination if I were dead. I figured that God would rather have me dead than continue to live in such gross sin. After my suicide mission failed, because I didn't have the heart to end it all and because part of me wanted to live even as an abomination, I decided to "repent" of my "sin." After an appropriate period of private repentance, I tearfully admitted to my best friend at the time who was a missionary that

PART 1: REJECTION

I had once been a lesbian. It was a very painful thing for me to admit and I wasn't sure she would forgive me even though God supposedly had. I became a poster child for the ex-gay movement in my small circle of churches. I claimed to have been an ex-lesbian because that is how I understood myself at the time. I hadn't even heard of bisexuality. But my whole life I had heard that being gay or lesbian, or "homosexual" or "queer" as it was called in our house, was the worst sin you could commit against God.

This meant that I wasn't just a sinner; I was the worst sinner that ever lived because I had been in relationships with women. I deserved to be cast out of my family and the church, to be put to death and then burn in hell forever because nobody who was LGBT was apparently a Christian. So despite the fact that I had "been saved" over and over again, it obviously didn't stick because I had been a lesbian. I was a disgusting piece of trash that wasn't worthy of God's love.

I came to find out you can't actually pray the gay away. When I realized that, I grudgingly admitted that I was bisexual. I thought that it was one thing to be bisexual, but it was still sin to be in relationships with women. In other words, I was still broken and still disgusting but as long as I didn't act on it I could maybe be at the bottom of God's totem pole rather than not being on it at all. I was upset with God because I couldn't figure out why I had to be bisexual and all the straight people had it easy. I didn't know why I had been given such a burden and I wished I could figure out what made me bisexual.

Then came the lowest point of my entire life. My husband, who I had married as part of my repentance, had cheated on me with multiple women. My children were taken away by the state for a mistake that he made. When it was so dark and I couldn't see through the dark I had to cling to the light of the world, which is Jesus. As I clung to Jesus, I began to be closer to him. As the darkness began to dissipate, I realized that God had created me to be bisexual and living that out would mean that God was delighted because God had handcrafted me that way. God made me bisexual, so it pleased God when I lived out my sexuality in full integrity.

I could finally be at peace with being bisexual, knowing that God created me that way and the Bible says that God looked at humankind and said that our creation was "very good." God created me. God created my sexuality as part of me. God made me bisexual because God thought that it was very good to do so. I needed to accept myself the way that God crafted me. God thought that I was very good.

At the lowest part of my life I found peace with being bisexual. I was twenty-eight years old. I had just left fundamentalism and was attending an Episcopal Church, which was and has been very healing for me. I was drawn to liturgical worship at a time when my soul was starved and I needed the Eucharist. Consuming Jesus in the Eucharist made me realize that God loved me and that I was a special creation of God's—that the verse about being fearfully and wonderfully made isn't just a verse for pro-lifers to use in their fight against abortion but that it was true for me. I was fearfully and wonderfully made as a special creation. It's been healing to be in a church where my sexuality is affirmed. Some people don't have that luxury.

I no longer have to hide myself from God and from the church, because who I am is a delight to the one who made me. I'm in a denomination that celebrates who I am, which is a huge blessing. I now have friends who accept me as a bisexual woman and their sister in Christ. I can be thankful that God created me this way and I'm assured of God's love for me. I'm not an abomination. I'm a beautiful woman created in God's image to worship God.

I still have scars from the crimson river. I have covered some of them up with a tattoo that says "grace," because God's grace kept me alive when I tried to end it all. I have a large crucifix tattooed to my left shoulder to have Jesus close to my heart and to remember that God made me who God wanted me to be, and that I need to live out that reality in my life, because that is how to please God.

Katy-Anne Binstead is a single mom to four kids, a happy liberal, and a committed Episcopalian. She grew up in Australia but now has US citizenship. She is currently studying for a Master of Arts in English and Creative Writing at Southern New Hampshire University and holds a Bachelor of Arts (honors) from CQ University Australia.

Intentionally Woven

Isaac Archuleta

My father spent every second of his leisure hours building a clubhouse for me the summer I turned eleven. I would stand from inside the house watching him labor away, wondering why he didn't want my company. I wanted nothing more than to matter to my father. I wanted him to see me as a spectacular version of a boy, so much so that I would captivate his heart, like any good son. But each nail he hammered was another nail in the coffin. From behind the windowpane, I could hear the echoes of the hammer reverberating through the house. I took his silence as panging rejection. To him, I didn't matter, or so I thought.

Years later, he was preaching in the church he had started in the basement of our small home. The tone of this particular sermon left panic booming within my chest—sinners, most precisely the homosexuals, would go to hell. He told us they would burn because they *made* God angry. When my father delivered this sermon I was a senior in high school. I had already lost my virginity to my high school sweetheart, Victoria. I loved Victoria very much and found our sexual rendezvous to be thrilling and deeply satisfying, but I was also attracted to the same gender. I hid my attractions for the same gender, not because I was embarrassed, but because outing myself, especially to my parents meant that I was a failed boy—a damaged son.

After trying to please God and my parents by fulfilling the Christian list of moral standards, my body betrayed me. I couldn't control the responses of my heart and sexuality. It wasn't as though I had *done* something wrong. It was that I *was* something wrong, damaged from the deepest core of my being. Even my innocent desires to love and be loved were disordered.

I drove home from church one afternoon with tears flowing down my cheeks and dripping from my chin. Although I had prayed everyday since the age of nine, asking God to take away my femininity and attractions for other boys my age, I was still broken. God didn't want to or couldn't help me. I was told that if I had shown God my seriousness and determination that he could take any discomfort from my life or any distortion from my emotional body. So I fasted two meals every day for my entire senior year of high school. When my attractions persisted I gave up on God.

Surely I had done everything I could to make God happy with me. I interpreted God's despondence as rejection. I was sixteen years old with a pit in my stomach that left me feeling utterly valueless. As a means to soothe the debilitating sense of failure and hopelessness, I began drinking. During the last semester of my high school career, I reached blackout drunk three times a week. My parents never knew.

Psychology quickly grabbed my attention in college and I soaked in its lessons. I was desperately trying to fix myself. And when the undergraduate courses left me more hungry than full, I applied for a master's program at a local seminary. I was going to become a professional Christian counselor. It was in seminary that I gave God one last chance to fix the broken person that I was.

Promising myself to find healing, I spent days and months in the library researching anything my eyes could graze pertaining to human sexuality. If I could find the answers to fix my broken sexuality, I would surely help fix all of the other gay and lesbian people in the world. But my research only led to more anger and self-hatred. After studying human development and sexuality I was devastated to find an inherent process that all humans undergo. We are all born with a fixed temperament, a specific gene code, and a particular familial environment. My seminary professors used to claim that God had knit me in my mother's womb. With fury, I would question God. He knew the home in which I would be born. He knew what temperament I would have and the genes that would eventually express themselves. He had the master plan for who I would become. He set me up to be a damaged, broken boy and a failed sinner and I had no choice in the matter. After sitting in counseling classes and reading several research articles in the library, I would drive home in rage. I would scream at God for picking me to be so despicable, especially when all I had ever craved to be and after all I had done to achieve value. I was not important to God. I would still burn in hell.

PART 1: REJECTION

As faithful Christians we are taught that we can control God's emotions with our behavior. If we are moral and righteous and behave perfectly we will *keep* God happy. If we sin, we make God mad. Such a message is passed down from the pulpit to the congregation, from parents to children, and from seminary professor to graduating minister. We have created an illusion that it is only by our good behavior that the almighty God remains pleased. What a backwards understanding of "God is love" (1 John 4:8) we preach. In fact, in counseling psychology we call this the illusion of control and it is one of the major pillars of codependency.

For most of my childhood I practiced the illusion of control as though it was my salvation. I believed that if I prayed everyday, fasted two meals a day in high school, sang at church, read my Bible, and treated my neighbor with love that God would have no choice but to reward me by taking away my attractions for men. When the illusion had finally proved itself as a farce, I was incredibly relieved.

When we live as someone who internalizes the truth of their creative design we drop the facades and we turn off our performances. We shed the illusion of control and begin speaking authentically with the actions of our lives. We are not ashamed to show just how God intentionally wove our personhood into being. We are confident and steadfast because we understand that reflecting God and expressing God's creativity means being our most authentic self for all time in front of all people.

It was during one of those car rides home from seminary, with angry tears falling down my face, that I realized something: if God is love—the experience, development, feeling, and expression of love—then there cannot be a clean version of God and a dirty version of God. In other words, if God *is* love, there is not a righteous version of love and a sinful version of love. Every form of *love* had to be God. I began to trust that my love was pure, no matter to whom it was directed and no matter from whom it was given. When I fell in love, with a man or a woman, I was experiencing and expressing God.

Several years later, I began to realize, as a faithful Christian, seminary professor, professional counselor, and a devoted follower of Christ, that I was intentionally woven in my mother's womb after all (Ps 139:13). God wanted me in that home, with this temperament, and these genes! My love wasn't dirty. I was supposed to be this man. No longer do I hear the echoing panic of nails trapping my personality into a coffin of self-hatred. I am free to show up just as God intends.

You see, it is not our job to convince God to love us. It is God's desire to convince us that we are loved—for who we are, not who we can become. This is the opposite of the illusion of control and we call it unconditional love.

Isaac Archuleta, MA, LPC, is the Interim Executive Director of the Gay Christian Network, a professional counselor, and former seminary professor who founded iAmClinic.org, a Denver-based counseling practice devoted to the LGBTQ community and their religious parents. In 2016, Isaac cofounded iAmProject, a nonprofit that specializes in repairing the intersection where sexuality, spirituality, and relationships meet. Being an ethnic and sexual minority, professional clinician, and a Christian, Isaac considers it his life's work to address the socioreligious mechanisms that mitigate psychological and spiritual development. Isaac is often heard on various podcasts and can be found throughout the country speaking at religious and counseling psychology conferences. Isaac hosts regional trainings for clergy and psychotherapists, contributes to *The Huffington Post*, and his work at iAmProject has been featured on National Public Radio. For more information, visit IsaacArchuleta.com.

Despair, Hope, and Renewal

A Cord of Three Strands

Rev. Courtney Barnes

There isn't any feeling quite like it: despair. It darkens any room you are in into a bleak, hopeless landscape punctuated with fears, which grow to dominate, loom large, and oppress. Despair wraps its tendrils painfully around your heart and climbs, creeping like a dark oppressive cancer through every vein. You can't breathe, you can't sleep, you can't eat. Your head pounds with a hollow sorrow so loud the only way to silence the voice saying, "you are worthless," is to kill yourself. You cry until you have no tears left. It's driving you; you are being driven to death by a depression so ferocious that it won't stop until your heart does. This is what it's like to commit suicide. Several months ago I was forced to resign from a ministry I loved and labored over for years because of bullying I suffered due to my bisexual orientation and non-binary gender identity. I took my cincture, a white braided rope tasseled on both ends with a knot that is used to tie the alb around my waist, and made a noose to hang myself. The only reason I'm still alive is that the metal bar in my closet began to bend under the weight of my body. If the closet bar were wooden I would have died. Mental illness, the devastating unseen damage caused by the cruelty of the church toward LGBTQ people is occurring in epidemic proportions. Forty percent of LGBTQ youth will attempt suicide.

When I came out to my family of origin, they disowned me. Coming to terms with my bisexuality has taken me all of my life. That is one reason the worst thing someone could say to a bisexual person is "you are just confused" or "you're just going through a phase." By the time a loved one has worked up enough courage to tell you, they are very certain. It was a long time before I could admit my orientation to myself, let alone find the courage to share this truth with anyone else. I was taught from a young age that same-sex attraction was wrong; it is sin. During my early child-hood I realized that although I was born female, I was different from other girls. I enjoyed playing basketball with the boys. I preferred wearing pants instead of dresses. I enjoyed fishing and climbing trees. I liked to play with my action figures and my Mr. T Doll. Barbies were pretty and I admired them, but I never identified with them. When I was in fifth grade, a female friend and I went to try on formal wear for an upcoming dance at the Boys and Girls Club. We went to the makeup counter at a department store and the clerk put eye shadow and eyeliner on my eyes. I'd never worn makeup before. When she was finished putting the eye shadow on my upper lids, she blew the excess eye shadow from my face and it was at that moment I developed my first crush on a female. I felt a strong sense of attraction to her. I didn't know what to call it, so I never told anyone. I remember this day very clearly. I was eleven years old.

What I had been taught about homosexuality by my family created a real sense of shame and so I avoided even thinking about my orientation, let alone learning about it. After many years of struggling silently with my orientation, I was able to come to terms with my faith and my sexuality. Knowing that this was the way God made me was key. Lady Gaga's song "Born This Way" actually helped me to accept myself: "God makes no mis-takes," she sang. Those lyrics resonated and were a comfort at a time when all I felt was turmoil. It was the first time I heard God portrayed as accept-ing. My upbringing taught me that God would reject me for being LGBTQ. I'd fought so long and hard against my orientation I had no idea that God made me this way and accepted me and my sexuality. I think that the deep-est fear LGBTQ people have is that their orientation is somehow a mis-take, that they are a mistake. Hearing for the first time in a song that God doesn't make mistakes gave me permission to come out and be myself. I was twenty-nine when I finally came out. I had been living with knowledge of my bisexual identity for eighteen years at that point. I'm thirty-six, so it has been twenty-five years that I've known about this facet of my identity. It has been difficult throughout my life trying to hide this part of myself from others. I hid my orientation out of a deep fear of being judged and rejected.

I'd known since earliest puberty I was attracted to both males and females. I've never fit into the traditional female look: I have very short hair like a man and I dress androgynously. When I came out at the age of twenty-nine, my mother showed open disgust for my orientation and my younger sisters distanced themselves from me. I got the cold shoulder and some open hostility I was not expecting. This caused a wound so deep that I can't easily bring myself to write about it. To have your loved ones reject you is possibly the worst pain imaginable. If you have never experienced this, then it's impossible to imagine. Familial rejection is a type of death. You become an orphan. It was like waking up one day and everyone you love is dead, except they aren't dead; you are dead to them and they just go on with their lives as if you never existed. It makes you wish you'd never been born. It makes you wish you could just die. I was badly abused by my family of origin and so letting go of them was painful but cathartic. I needed the distance in order to build a healthy life for myself. My husband and I moved across the country to another state with our three children and started over. It was the best thing we've ever done. Severing those toxic connections to people who could not accept me for who I am was liberating. This created the space in my life to find my true calling and pursue it. The only thing I regret now is not having left sooner.

As a bisexual person, monogamously married for sixteen years to my husband Kevin and a parent of three school-age children, I often find myself misunderstood when I confide that I am bisexual. When I say, "I'm bisexual," I am often met with misunderstanding, judgment, bullying, and shunning from the Christian community. This has been both alienating and disheartening because this is the way God made me. I didn't choose it. I've often wished I could just be straight. I tried for many years to deny my same-sex attraction and pretend I was straight, but the voice of my own truth grew louder and louder. When a friend of our family came out and confided in me that he is gay, something broke. I saw how cruel people were, how they distanced themselves from him after they knew. I saw the pain his family was in at the way he was treated. I saw the persecution and unfair discrimination other LGBTQ people are facing both inside and outside of the church and it broke my heart. I realized that by default, my silence was contributing to the invisibility of LGBTQ people. I realized that I needed to be brave and have the integrity to admit who I am to others and myself. I realized how important it was that I be honest about my orientation, so I could help create awareness. I wanted to become an advocate and make my voice heard so that I could help the church to understand. I've done that and I've never looked back. I am an LGBTQ rights advocate in my community. I volunteer regularly for TIHAN: Tucson Interfaith HIV/ AIDS Network. I recently walked with AIDS Ribbon Tucson along with many other LGBTQ members of the community at the Pride Parade. I use my ministry page and my home page on social media to advocate equality and acceptance for the LGBTQ community.

My belief is that sexuality exists on a spectrum. Kinsey created a numeric scale to measure sexual orientation. Labels cannot adequately define any one person. Sexuality has also been described as fluid and able to change over time. Being married to a man does not negate my capacity to be attracted to a woman. I just met the right man before I met the right woman. My orientation does not make me more likely to engage in a physical relationship with someone besides my spouse, although some bisexual people are polyamorous, which is fine if you are, but I'm not. Bisexual people are capable of monogamy as much as any straight person. Kevin and I have always been faithful to each other, that is just part of who we are.

When I've come out to friends, their responses have been both humiliating and disappointing. I've had friends pull away or reject me, or just stop speaking to me more often than not. It has been extremely hurtful. I had a best friend who wrongly assumed that my sexuality meant I was secretly attracted to her—and so she severed our friendship. Explaining gently that I wasn't attracted to her didn't help at all, it embarrassed her—and she stopped speaking to me. My orientation does not mean I am attracted to every man and woman I see, any more than a straight person is attracted to every person of the opposite gender they see. Woody Allen said, "Being bisexual just means you are twice as likely to get a date on a Friday night." That really isn't true. In fact, it's so far from being true, it is the opposite of what my experience has been. Being bisexual has led to many people misjudging me based on what they've seen or heard from the media or even watched in porn. I think most people's only "knowledge" of bisexuality is tragically misinformed by the porn industry. Just as straight porn is in no way indicative of what a loving heterosexual relationship is in reality; neither is bisexual porn indicative of what a bisexual person's orientation is or what their expression of sexuality is. In his song "Blackstar" David Bowie sang, "I'm not a porn star," and if you think hard enough about why he felt he had to sing that, it breaks your heart. He was bisexual and also married for much of his life to one partner—but was wrongfully assumed by many to be inherently promiscuous because of his orientation. People judge and wrongfully assume that being bisexual means that a person is a swinger or engages in threesomes or orgies, and I've never been a swinger or engaged in a threesome or an orgy. I'm a married person who has always been faithful to my spouse. Can you imagine how hurtful it is when a friend misinterprets your platonic affection for sexual attraction, once you confide your orientation? It feels like a betrayal. It feels like someone taking advantage of a confidence to malign you for being their friend. It makes you wish you had never trusted the person enough to be honest with them. It feels like being wrongfully accused of something.

Coming out has been so lonely and so isolating that I recommend being extremely selective with whom you share your orientation, especially if you sense that you will be ostracized for it. If a person displays bigoted attitudes toward others, do not wrongly assume that they won't also treat you similarly. I've found the way a person treats others is a good predictor of how they will treat you. And if you are a young person living at home, dependent on your parents for support, I recommend waiting until you are on your own to come out. You could be thrown out on the streets or physically hurt. There is nothing brave about telling people your orientation if you know they will be hostile toward you. And that's not to say that if you do receive a hostile or even violent reaction from someone that it was in any way your fault; far from it. I'm just advocating caution. Sometimes staying silent about your orientation so that you can survive is the bravest thing you can do. And that should be your primary goal as a young LGBTQ person: to stay alive and to stay safe. Don't come out until you feel safe and you feel the time is right for you. Only you can decide when that is. A sobering reality is that 40 percent of homeless youth are LGBTQ and they are the most preyed upon group of children in the world, often falling victim to people who exploit them in human trafficking and prostitution.

After several years on the pastoral care team of our church, ministering to the sick of our congregation, working in a hospice as a chaplain on a volunteer basis, and running several ministries, I'd finished a long and taxing discernment process and was accepted as a postulant for holy orders in the Episcopal Church to become an ordained deacon. This was a several-year commitment, and I founded a sewing and quilting guild to teach women to sew. We made quilts for Project Linus, a ministry that distributes the quilts to children who have cancer or who are in the foster care system. I also was a eucharistic minister in the Episcopal Church, serving on a regular basis at the altar several times a week. I was active on the military affairs committee. I served as indigenous ministries liaison, in an outreach to the indigenous community. I was also a junior in college in the Bachelor of Psychology program, working toward my degree in psychology to become a hospice chaplain. This is a calling I've felt all my life. Receiving the church's approval for ordination was, as I thought at the time, the fulfillment of the calling and a reward for all of the hard work I'd done. I made many sacrifices to be accepted. I was elated that I finally had the opportunity to follow my calling to be a chaplain.

I came out in 2009 to family and friends, but publicly to my church in the process of my discernment. Some people were very supportive, some shunned and excluded me, and some bullied me. The looks I've gotten of withering contempt and disdain in the church have been very hurtful. The inherent lack of respect many people have for LGBTQ people, especially young people, combined with ignorance about bisexuality created a hostile climate in my church. The bullying got so bad that I was eventually forced to resign. When most people hear that I resigned from a position of ministry in the Episcopal Church, they are often shocked because the Episcopal Church's stated policy is one of full inclusion. That may be their stated policy, but that is not what I experienced in our congregation and that was not what they practiced. I was marginalized, excluded, and rarely if ever given credit for my contributions in ministry. I saw people promoted over me who had less experience, while I was forced to resign. The only reason for this mistreatment is because I am bisexual. This is why I have emphasized the necessity of being cautious about who you come out to.

I'd been sent to counseling when the diocese read I'd suffered abuse and a fellow clergy member wrongly accused me of not taking their criticism well as a result of the abuse I suffered. This was made up to get rid of me. This meant that in order to be ordained I would have had to go to counseling indefinitely. The clergy member who lied about me knew how painful talking about the abuse I suffered was for me and that this would likely end my plans for ordination if I was required to talk about it on a regular basis. The pain of talking about the abuse I suffered as a child triggered my PTSD and it made proceeding with ordination impossible. I refused the counseling as I felt they were more interested in controlling me and grinding down my personality to fit into a servile role they envisioned for me, rather than empowering me for the ministry I am called to by God. I left heartbroken, confused, and dejected.

At this low point I sunk into a deep depression and decided that life was no longer worth living. When my suicide attempt failed, I got into bed and cried. I survived the coming months of despair somehow, and emerged despairing but still alive. During this time, my only comfort was to pray that somehow God could restore my situation and help me survive. I couldn't imagine how he could restore any part of the dream of fulfilling my calling as a board certified hospice chaplain without ordination, which is a requirement for certification with the Association of Professional Chaplains.

After a time of prayer and seeking, I decided to continue with my plans to become a priest and I was accepted to Chicago Theological Seminary where I was given a scholarship and made a student ambassador. This is the fulfillment of my calling and the missing piece of the puzzle I still needed to become a chaplain.

What hurt me most about the Episcopal Church was that the terms they set forth were so oppressive they made it impossible for me to be ordained. I strongly believe it was due to my orientation and that was the real reason I was forced out of my postulancy. If I hadn't resigned I would have had to subject myself to abusive ongoing counseling, and so I decided it just wasn't worth the deep pain that would cause me. Since then, God has brought things full circle and restored to me not only my ministry but my hope for the future.

I believe that God can redeem any situation, no matter how painful. Even if it seems you've been abandoned by those you love or rejected by your family, or that you've lost an important opportunity just for being yourself, know that God witnesses your pain. When someone draws a line and denies someone else justice, God moves to stand on the other side of that line with the person they have excluded. God has been my strength and my comfort through so many losses and has restored to me my calling and my dream of becoming a chaplain. My ministry is Spectrum Hospice Chaplaincy. I minister to Alzheimer's and dementia patients through my interfaith services. Bringing hope, comfort, and love to people whom society often neglects and ignores during the process of their death is the focus of my ministry. I am grateful to God that I can continue to live and serve him and his people.

This week I walked across the stage of University of Arizona's Honors Convocation to receive my honors cord, an award for making the Dean's List the past year: a white rope with tassels at both ends. It struck me how very similar it was to the noose I made of my cincture that I almost took my own life with. My honors cord symbolizes new life and hope. I will wear it when I graduate summa cum laude in May of 2017 with my Bachelor of Arts in Psychology. Earning my Master of Divinity through Chicago Theological Seminary is the next step of my journey and a fulfillment of my hopes for the future.

Don't give up on your dreams just because people judge you unfairly or reject you for who you are. Even if you can't foresee how God will use the pain in your life, God can transform the pain of your rejection and bring you restoration and social justice that maybe you cannot even imagine right now. He literally turned my noose into an honors cord, and my broken dreams into a renewal. Instead of becoming a deacon, which is a priest's assistant, I'm now a minister with a thriving outreach. If that's not social justice, then I don't know what is. If you've come out and received rejection from your faith community and family, take heart in knowing that God loves you unconditionally and accepts you. Trust that he will bring things full circle. An unbreakable strength will be woven of the despair, hope, and renewal you experience. The body of Christ needs you and your gifts. Remember that there is a place for you in this world. No matter how hurt and broken you are right now, please don't give up.

Rev. Courtney Barnes is a chaplain providing compassionate end-of-life spiritual care to patients with terminal illness through her ministry Spectrum Hospice Chaplaincy. She is a writer advocating for social justice for the LGBTQ community. Her outreach has included interfaith communion services for Alzheimer's dementia patients, fundraising for TIHAN: Tucson Interfaith HIV/AIDS Network, pioneering efforts to benefit terminally ill children, serving as a translator for a nonprofit surgical team that donates free and low cost surgeries, and administrating a support group for people with autoimmune disease. Courtney is a Master of Divinity student at Chicago Theological Seminary. She is a graduate of the University of Arizona, where she studied psychology and philosophy. She and her husband Kevin are raising three children together.

You Belong

Avery Belyeu

"God please help me not be gay." I said that prayer, or some variation of it, on an almost daily basis starting at around twelve years old. I prayed it when I went to bed at night, and when I woke up in the morning, and often in the middle of the day. Sometimes I even prayed it silently to myself as I sat next to my family on Sunday morning at the local Kingdom Hall of Jehovah's Witnesses. Sometimes I even thought about trying to make a bargain with God—I mean we have examples of that in the Bible, right? "So God, I will do anything you want me to for the rest of my life if you just help me not be gay. Anything."

Eventually I stopped praying. I don't remember when it happened exactly. It was more of a slow gradual process I think. I didn't stop being involved with my local congregation of Jehovah's Witnesses though. To the contrary, I was more active than ever. At sixteen I became a Regular Pioneer, an appointed position given to someone who spends seventy hours a month evangelizing in the local community. And at eighteen I was appointed as a ministerial servant, the equivalent of a deacon in many other churches, and I gave my first Sunday sermon to a packed church. Looking back, I think that I felt that if I did everything just right, if I was the model young person, then God would eventually fix whatever this thing was that was wrong with me.

But it didn't work out that way. As the years went by the depression and feelings of loneliness and isolation increased. I couldn't find a way to reconcile the teachings of my congregation and the things I believed to be true and who I was deep down inside. I felt like a liar. A fake. A fraud. Those feelings eventually brought me, at twenty-two years old, to the side of a mountain on the Blue Ridge Parkway, right outside West Jefferson, North Carolina. I pulled up to one of the mountain overlooks and sat on the side of a rocky ledge looking down at the green rolling hills thousands of feet below me. I had decided I was going to jump. Because I had really tried everything and I still wasn't any different than when I said that first prayer at twelve years old. And I knew that if my congregation found out I would be disfellowshipped. I'd lose my church family, and worse than that I would lose my parents and my siblings too. My family would be disgraced, ashamed, embarrassed, and so disappointed in me. So I decided to jump. It was just going to be easier that way.

But then I decided to pray. Just one last time I would pray. Looking back now this is when I remember that I hadn't prayed in a really long time. Starting that prayer felt like trying to start an engine in an old rusty car. It wasn't easy. But I looked out across the mountains and I prayed, "God, I know we haven't talked in a long time, but listen I really need you to show up right now. And I don't just need a pat on the head. I need more than that—OK? I know you don't do signs or anything anymore but I really need something here. I need to know that you don't hate me for being who I am." And as I prayed these words I looked over to my left and a deer and a fawn came walking out of the woods. They walked up so close I could have touched them. Then they froze and just looked at me with their big brown eyes. In my mind the meaning was immediate. It was as if I heard God speak and say, "I couldn't ever hate you anymore than this deer could hate this little fawn. You are perfectly made. I love you just the way you are. And you are a part of all of this. You belong here." Slowly the deer and the fawn turned around and went back into the woods. I sat there for a few moments, stunned, and then I got up, got in my car, and drove back down the mountain.

That day was just the start of a very long journey. I did come out and I was disowned by my family and rejected by my church and the extended family that represented. The following few years were hard. Very hard. For awhile I said I was agnostic, then atheist. No matter what I said though, in my heart I was always tethered to what happened on the side of the mountain that day. I knew that my journey with faith wasn't done. Eventually, I found my way to an Episcopal Church. And it was in that place that I found community again. I was healed by the balm of the Eucharist and the rhythm of the liturgy calmed my mind and comforted my heart. I received masterful pastoral care from a wonderful and caring priest. And most importantly, I learned how to pray again.

Eventually I found my way into suicide prevention as a line of work. And that was when I learned that my experience of feeling hopeless and alone isn't unique for young LGBTQ people and sadly those feelings are often worse for young people in religious homes. I learned that LGBTQ youth are four times more likely to attempt suicide than straight youth. And youth who experience severe family rejection like I did are eight times more likely that their fellow LGBTQ peers to attempt suicide. I also learned that LGBTQ youth make up a staggering 40 percent of the youth homeless population in the United States. The research told me why, and told me how many, but it didn't have to tell me how any of this felt because I already knew. I lived it.

A few years after I started my career in suicide prevention, I was living in New York City and traveling a lot for work. My travels took me to a rural college in the South where I facilitated a workshop about LGBTQ folks and suicide prevention. A lot of the college students in the room were very emotional during the presentation. Many of them were having a hard time coming out. At the end of the presentation a young woman came up to me and told me her story. With tears running down her face she described her struggle of coming out to her religious family. I knew what she was going through. I reached out and put my hand on her shoulder and said the words that I'd heard that day on the mountainside, "You are perfectly made and God loves you just as you are." She looked up at me a little stunned and said, "No one has ever said that to me before. Thank you!" I think it was at that moment I knew that at some point in the future I would have to find a way to merge my suicide prevention career with church ministry.

Fast forward about five years and I came out again. After years of processing I finally found the courage to declare that "gay" isn't really the right word to describe who I am and I came out fully as a transgender woman. But this time coming out is different. This time I have a community of people surrounding me who are companions on this new journey—companions who know how important it is to look deep into my eyes and tell me, "You are beautiful. You are perfectly made. God loves you exactly as you are."

My journey has also taken me to a progressive seminary where I am learning to integrate my passion for public health and mental health with sound theology—theology that liberates and heals.

I have begun to form a new prayer that I pray almost daily, but it's a different than what I prayed when I was twelve years old. I pray for a church that will put the law of love before doctrines about gender and sexuality. I pray for a church that will open its arms wide and embrace the outcast and care for the wounded. I lift up my hands and I pray for all the young LGBTQ people who are trying to discern how to reconcile who they know they are with what they hear from the pulpit each Sunday. I pray for them to have hope, courage, and resilience no matter what may come. And I pray that if and when those young LGBTQ folks face the hardship of rejection from their church and family that there will be a church on every corner that opens its doors wide to care for the wounds, to pray for healing, and to look deeply into the eyes of that young person and say, "You are beautiful, you are perfectly made. God loves you *exactly* as you are. You are welcome here. You are part of all of this. You belong."

Avery Belyeu is a transgender educator, suicide prevention practitioner, and aspiring theologian. She is a second year Master of Divinity student and Haggard Legacy Fellow at Brite Divinity School. She's a national expert on LGBTQ youth, suicide prevention, and youth homelessness. She has worked at the Trevor Project and currently works in suicide prevention for a national suicide prevention organization based in Washington, DC. Avery currently serves on the advisory boards for the Runaway and Homeless Youth Training and Technical Assistance Center as well as Trans Lifeline, a suicide prevention lifeline serving the needs of the transgender community.

Liberated

Michael Vazquez

Fall 2014. The leaves were changing colors. The mountain air was crisp. Something new was coming.

I was a campus minister with InterVarsity Christian Fellowship/USA staffing our annual fall gathering of students in Utah and Southern Idaho. It was the culmination of our initial push to reach new students on campus at the beginning of the academic year. At this conference, we hoped students would walk away having heard about the love of Jesus. Students would hear about how we believed that Jesus is in constant loving pursuit of them. That he desires their transformation. That he had something new and something deeply good for them.

Every year we would talk to students about Jesus' interaction with Peter and the others on the boat in the Gospel of Luke. We would talk about the beauty of following Jesus. We would challenge them about what we believed it meant to follow Jesus. We would teach that following Jesus meant that Jesus gets to have control over all areas of our life: our time, our money, our education—and our bodies. Saturday night, we took the students back to the story of the men in the boat. We told them, in pretty typical evangelical fashion, that they were, in fact, not in the boat with Jesus, but instead, they were drowning. We'd tell them that their sin and addictions and character flaws were all pointing to the fact they desperately needed Jesus. We'd dim the lights, play emotionally provoking acoustics, while calling them all to give their lives over to following Jesus. Some students would stand and make a commitment to follow Jesus. We'd celebrate. The next morning we'd talk about what we believed a Jesus-centered community should look like. After that we'd send everyone home until we did it again the next year. Simple.

However, for me it wasn't so simple this year. Change had come and was knocking loudly. After the call to faith, although students were dismissed for the night, they were invited to stay for extended musical worship and prayer ministry—this was a critical transaction for many students. They would come with their petitions or seek inner healing for a litany of pain and trauma, or sin and addictions. They wanted to be "better" followers of Jesus, and prayer ministry was the key to make that happen.

One of these students showed up as an arbiter for change in my life. He was the fifth or sixth student I had led through prayer ministry that night. At that point, I was in awe of what I had seen so far. Students were experiencing emotional healing and walking away feeling profoundly transformed. It was a beautiful night. I was so proud of the work we were doing. I believed we were changing lives for good. As the night went on, I was tired but filled with joy and awe—at least until I spoke with this student. He came to me and told me he was unsure what to do with about his sexuality. He identified as a cisgender gay male. He told me about his struggle with reconciling his faith and his sexuality. He expressed feeling as if God was not displeased with him nor condemning him for being gay. However, that didn't coincide with the messages he was receiving from his campus ministers (my coworkers), his friends in the ministry, or the church at large. He didn't feel ostracized by his community, he just wanted to know what was right and good—he just wanted to be faithful. What he was hearing was that to pursue a relationship with another man was to live into his broken sexual identity. Still uncertain, he'd come to me, specifically, for direction, as it was common knowledge I'm gay and was always open to talking with students who were in the midst of processing the intersection of their faith and sexual orientation.

Although I knew it was tearing me apart inside, I was fully committed to the evangelical posture on homosexuality and broader LGBT issues. I held to what InterVarsity would soon name "redeemed sexuality"—a theological posture that viewed same-sex attraction and the complexity of LGBT issues as a result of the fall, and thus, outside of God's plan. From the vantage point of onlookers, I was an icon of redeemed sexuality. I had convinced myself that this was the best choice for my life. I had left behind my sexuality in order to faithfully follow Jesus. I became a full time minister of the Gospel. It was the perfect story. I had become a poster child for living "redeemed sexuality."

This student came to me because I was embodying evangelicalism's exalted picture of a redeemed gay man. He hoped for "healing" that would allow him to raise a family; but, if not, he sought to have the courage and strength to live celibate for the rest of his life. We would pray and Jesus would free him from his sexual sin. It would be easy. It would be another success story I could toss into a newsletter to churches and donors in hopes of raising more financial support for the ministry. It was another success story that would confirm InterVarsity's view of sexuality. A view that I would eventually come to understand was toxic, abusive, and simply wrong.

I was the "success story." I had sat in a similar place at InterVarsity's Urbana Student Mission Conference in 2012. I had received the same kind of prayer ministry for the exact same reason. I walked away from that experience disoriented. I hadn't been healed. In fact, my prayer minister told me he felt God was saying I would never be healed. I don't think he realized the implications his words would have, but they radically altered my life. I gave up hope of having a family and tried to follow Jesus faithfully, even though my heart remained unsettled. I lied to myself endlessly that I was okay with this theology and the life it expected I would live.

The student and I prayed. We discerned. We sought Jesus. The student told me, "God is showing me a picture of me married and with a family."

I thought to myself, "Is it possible that God might actually heal him? I was told I could never be healed . . . but if he can . . . maybe . . ."

I asked him to share more. He smiled and told me he felt God was showing him a picture of him married to a man and, together, they were raising a child.

I tried to keep myself together. How do I shatter his hope? This obviously couldn't be from God. Every word had to be tested against Scripture, and Scripture is very clearly against homosexuality. Or is it?

I was disoriented again, and confused, but was trying to stay professional and pastoral. He, on the other hand, was elated and convinced of something that I hadn't even imagined—God was deeply pleased with him and, when it came to his sexual orientation, no healing was necessary.

I vaguely remember encouraging him to continue to ask God more questions and to let his community help him discern this further. My training as a campus minister and what naïve experience I presumed to have of the Divine, had not prepared me for that moment. I went home disoriented, confused, and bewildered, and sat in bed and cried.

I eventually got up, brushed my shoulders off, and began to search the Scriptures. I prayed, cried out to God, demanded answers, and cried some more. I studied contradicting theological texts, listened to major voices while leaning in to more obscure ones. I prayed more. I fasted. I sought counsel and community. I demanded more answers. I read more books. I cried again. I sought more voices. I prayed even more. I found additional mentors and teachers. I cried some more still. I demanded answers.

The answers came faster than I thought. Swift like the change that comes with the fall. The spring of 2015 brought them along with the refreshing fragrance of new life: God was uniquely and divinely pleased with me, and required no healing of my sexual orientation. Instead, God offered full blessing of an abundant and liberated life as a gay Christian man. If I wanted, I could finally be free from the weight of shame, oppression, and repression. I could also be free from participating in the proliferation of this corrupt and deadly theology. My liberation also afforded me the strength to push back against the use of prayer, so-called "reparative" practices and toxic teachings by InterVarsity, and evangelicalism at large, to try and change students' sexual orientations and oppress sexual minorities.

Lamentably, it had not dawned on me that liberation was possible until I found myself in the very seat of the oppressor. In an interview with the BBC, Nigerian author Chimamanda Ngozie Adichie said, "Every system of oppression has people who are in the group of the oppressed that contribute to that oppression." Nothing could be truer of my lived experience as a professional minister of the Gospel. I embodied and testified to the very theology that inflicts violence against the dignity and humanity of LGBTQ persons who, in the very nature of their created beings, are fully dignified children of God. This violence comes from a refusal to submit to the theological imperative of hospitality.

Genesis 18:1–8 is the beginning of a strange narrative of a visit of the Divine to Abraham and Sarah. Abraham, we are told, is sitting in the heat of the day in the shade of the entrance to his tent. His countenance is lifted and he sees three men. What happens upon Abraham's gaze falling on these strange visitors is quite astonishing. Abraham was able to immediately acknowledge that the Divine had shown up in his midst—the image of God had arrived on his doorstep. His response, and that of Sarah and their servant, was to quickly move into hosting the image of God as lavishly as possible. Abraham appears to long for nothing but that the presence of the Lord would not move on from his dwelling yet. "If I have found favor in your eyes, my Lord, do not pass your servant by" (v. 3). Abraham sets before the Lord a feast, a meal much more lavish than originally offered. The text says that while the visitors ate, Abraham simply "stood near them" (v. 8).

This text is rich with meaning, and the implications of the text are profoundly prophetic. Abraham was able to see the image of God approaching. His response, and arguably the only appropriate response to seeing the image of God approach, was to throw a lavish feast.

How do we respond when we see the image of God approach us? Unfortunately, it depends. Although we acknowledge that we are all God's image bearers, we have taken it upon ourselves as the evangelical church to determine who fully bears the Divine image and who does not. This act strips away the dignity of those we have categorized as only being a partial or damaged image bearer. We have done this to the LGBT community in such a way that, when an LGBT person is brave enough to shadow the entrances of our sanctuaries or halls of ministries, we are incapable of showing them radical and lavish hospitality. Instead, seeing them as incomplete, damaged, or dangerous, we offer them pity, disdain, flat out ignore them, or even curse them for our perception of them. We prepare no feast for them and never stand near enough to them to actually be present in their lives, their stories, and their lived experiences—all of which would challenge our worldviews and theologies.

Genesis 18 is an invitation. First, it is an invitation to repentance. We need to repent of the ways in which we have taken the role of God in ascribing dignity via His image, bestowing it only on those who look like us, live like us, love like us. We need to surrender that power back to the God—who created all in the Divine image and called it very good. It is an invitation to repent of our refusal to host the image of God when it arrives on our doorsteps.

Second, it is an invitation into action. The story is a constant stream of motion ensuring that all the needs of the Lord are met lavishly. Likewise, I believe it is our theological imperative to see the image of God in all, especially in the lives of the most marginalized and oppressed. As the image of God draws near to us, we are invited to move rapidly into full inclusion and celebration of the bearer of the image of God.

Finally, it is an invitation to be present and listen. As Abraham waits on the Lord in verse 8, I believe we also are called to wait on those who bear God's image—to be present to their presence, to their needs, to their stories. In doing so, I believe that we will move away from perpetuating the violence of theologies that do not affirm the full inclusion of LGBT individuals and the queer community at large.

Living out the reality of my own oppression, I never fully hosted students like the one who approached me for prayer that night. As hostile as it was to my soul, as detrimental as it was to my well-being, I embodied a theology and conviction that I was inherently damaged and unable to fully display the image of God in my broken humanity because I am gay. I perpetuated this violence because I, like my cisgender heterosexual family, did not know how to do the very basic things we see in this text. I did not know how to identify, see, and therefore acknowledge the image of God as it approached me. That led to me not being able to receive and lavishly host all those who bear the Divine image. It also did not allow me to be present with the God who is revealed in the life, presence, and story of those who radiantly carry God's image.

I am indebted to this student for transforming my capacity to see myself fully and bringing me to a place where I could experience my own liberation. I pray he was able to find his. In moving forward, I believe it is of the greatest importance that we critically evaluate ourselves and our spaces of worship. We need to ensure whether or not we are able to see, receive, and be present with the image of God revealed to us in LGBT people. It is crucial that we identify what it is that precludes us from lavishly hosting and celebrating that which God has already fully affirmed and dignified so we can move in a direction that fundamentally transforms our broken and prejudicial system of hosting into a theology and praxis of hosting that reflects the lavish hosting of God.

Would it be so, that justice and liberation would come to all who need freedom and the assurance of their Divine Radiance. Would it be so, Jesus.

Michael Vazquez is an imperatival force that has been rendered iridescent by time. Michael is a public theologian, activist, mystic, storyteller, and educator advocating for justice and liberation for all. Michael is also the founder of Brave Commons: An Inclusive Christian Campus Ministry.

Coming Out

Jennifer Hoffman

Throughout my four years in high school, I would have reoccurring dreams about dying. They weren't always the same dream, but they always had one of two themes. Sometimes I would die in a car accident, skidding off the road during a winter storm, hitting a tree or telephone pole. Other times I would be floating above my own funeral. These dreams happened so frequently and were so potent I started to believe that I wasn't going to live for very long. Somewhere along the way, I had made up my mind that twenty-five years old was the end mark of my existence. At that time, I had no idea why that number seemed relevant.

I grew up in a Catholic household. Not because we were strictly practicing, but because my father grew up in a Catholic home. To this day, my grandparents, who are in their nineties, still attend mass twice a week. I'm fairly certain my mother wanted us to follow in the same path, not because she was an overtly religious person, but because she grew up with an atheist father. My mother never speaks of God or faith. However, she has the word "believe" sprinkled around my parents' house as if leaving silent notes of love and faith for all to see. My entire life, I have subconsciously known nothing but to hope and believe in something greater, something higher. Maybe that belief is from all her sprinkling; maybe it has been the way my soul craves to know myself and what's around me that is deeper than what the eyes can see. I'm not really sure, but when I look back at my life, everything looks so much more intentional. I can see the way God has had His hands on me and moved through my life that I always just thought was coincidental.

I was baptized, received my first communion, and confirmed in a small Catholic church in my also very small hometown. I won't lie—I hated catechism. I didn't understand the stories because I couldn't relate to them. I always felt like I was being talked at, told what to do, what to believe, what to say, when to stand, when to kneel, and everything else in between. I have nothing against Catholicism. I have not a single doubt in my mind that everything God does is intentional. However, at the time, I wasn't interested. By the end of high school, prayer became this superficial use of making wishes to God as if He were a genie. Simultaneously, I was starting to realize that what I initially thought was looking up to women of the same sex because they were good at the sports I was playing was actually much more than that. The details of how and who helped me find that out are irrelevant. However, my first girlfriend was a story of confusion, heartbreak, and absolute fear of anyone finding out. It was, without a doubt, one of the most alone and frightening places in my life. Much of why I am who I am and why I find it necessary to own our stories is to be an example so no other child has to live in such fear or confusion while trying to find out who they are in world that doesn't give them the room to be authentically themselves.

To be clear, prior to my first girlfriend in high school, I didn't know what gay was. All I knew of being gay was Puck from the Real World and what I overheard adults saying about it being a sin in my church. One day, my girlfriend completely stopped talking to me—no warning, no letter, no explanation. To this day I have no idea what happened. We passed each other in the halls, had gym lockers next to each other in gym class, and passed each other in parties after that day, and she never said a single word to me. I have never been in that darkness and fear since that time my senior year in high school—asking who I was, what that even means, and not having a single person I felt comfortable enough to tell my story to. This is where I began to question if there could be a God at all. I was flooded with questions about this genie up above: Who would create me like this knowing the fear and pain I would live in daily? How did you make a mistake with me? Why is it so wrong with loving another human, regardless of their gender or identity?

For the next seven years, through college and a graduate program, the God of my catechism days became nothing more than a higher power that I believed used karma to deliver or restrict our lives. I believed bad things happen to good people because good people would use their pain, their weaknesses, their struggles, and their darkest days as a catalyst for change. I didn't know who or what that high power was, but I knew something was running this controlled chaos that I saw of the world.

PART 1: REJECTION

Shortly after I finished grad school, I started dating a woman who loved God in ways that made absolutely no sense to me. She was strong in her faith. Her church community was nothing like I understood of religion. The love that burned inside her for God turned everything I made my world of "faith" into upside down. For the first time in my life, my mother sprinkling "believe" around our house finally made sense when I heard my girlfriend talk about her faith. It was a handful of days before my twenty-fifth birthday when I asked this woman who gave a new meaning of religion to me, "How could God ever love me if I'm gay?" She took my hands and told me, "Sweetheart, you are not a mistake. God has never stopped loving you. All He has made you to be is out of love, and there is never a mistake in that." In that moment, the incessant dreams about death came true. I died when I turned twenty-five, because when those words spilled out of her mouth, it was the first time in my twenty-four years that I heard God. I was reborn.

Since then, my life has been an endless wandering through all these questions—never because I didn't know who I was, but from realizing that we are all constantly unfolding who we are and what we believe in. Faith and coming out are not destinations, but a journey to be lived through love and grace and a journey that opens us up more and more to our truest and highest selves. Faith has been like my coming out story—ongoing, constantly transforming, and always renewing with every experience and every human soul I encounter.

Jennifer Hoffman has recently relocated to California, where she now works as a Service Coordinator and Youth Program Leader at Palo Alto Housing. Prior to her relocation, she was a Certified Tobacco Treatment Specialist and Prevention Specialist for three years for Pittsburgh Mercy Health System in Pittsburgh, Pennsylvania. During her time in Pittsburgh, she also created LOCO Fitness, a venture that was designed to create an environment conducive to physical and spiritual growth. Jennifer's passion and desire to grow as a person translates into the relationships she builds with the children and adults she works with on a daily basis. In April 2017, Jennifer's passion of creating authentic spaces for people to share their truth gave her the opportunity to speak at TEDx Texas A&M. Her talk was titled "Authentic Truth Requires Authentic Spaces."

The Exorcism

Billy Kluttz

L ike many people, my journey to reconcile faith and identity began with an exorcism.

I grew up in a conservative evangelical Christian family in the southeastern United States. My parents were good and loving people—despite our differences of opinion on several matters of importance—but more on that later.

Decisions about my faith and identity arrived during high school. I came out to my mother at age sixteen in the upstairs of our suburban North Carolina home; it did not go well. I remember struggling to get the words out. I remember my mother on the floor, devastated and crying after I told her that I was gay. My only request was that she not tell my father when he got home; minutes later, she told him the news as he walked in the door.

That's when the exorcism happened. It wasn't one of the exciting, Hollywood-type exorcisms that you see on TV; the ones with spinning heads and well-trained priests. Rather, it was a sort of do-it-yourself, old-fashioned exorcism. Believing that an otherworldly force had convinced me that I was gay, my parents laid hands on me and prayed vigorously for Satan to leave my body. They attempted to cast out demons while I lay there on the floor.

That night, I realized that I was never going to have a typical coming out story; a cute anecdote you can share during small talk and first dates. But that night, on the floor of my childhood home, waiting for the prayers and tears to end, something changed.

I found Jesus that night, face down in the carpet of my childhood home. I heard the loud prayers above me, asking God to heal and forgive me. I heard the shouts of anger and sadness. But I also heard another voice simply saying "no." Above the commotion, I heard a voice telling me, "No. Don't believe it. Don't listen to this. Enough."

My journey toward self-acceptance did not take years of intense study and prayer. For me, reconciliation was not the result of the perfect logical argument or well-constructed syllogism. That's not my story.

My story is a relational one. I found Jesus during an exorcism. It was God's holy "no" that saved my life that night.

It is that same Holy Negation that keeps many LGBTQ folks alive. The taunts of street preachers, the distance of friends, the silence of family holiday dinners are survived only because of God's still, small voice saying, "No. This is ridiculous. Tune this out."

During seminary, I learned that there is a grand theological term for all of this sacred naysaying: apophatic theology. Apophatic, or negative, theology begins by describing what God is not in order to approach what God is.

It's great to have an academic term, but I still prefer God's holy "no."

It takes years (perhaps decades) of faithfully saying no before you can ever say yes; this is the first great truth of queer Christianity. The ancient Christian confessions ask us to begin with a long list of affirmations; queer Christians begin, instead, with our own liturgy of negation.

We say no to communities of hurt and harm. We reject theologies of transphobia, heterosexism, and cissexism. Maybe most difficult of all, we slowly learn to silence the sounds of self-hatred and doubt deep within our own souls.

Our theological story is one of tearing down and rebuilding. I think that is what excites me most about our moment in the church's history. After a generation of faithful negation and survival, we are on the cusp of a Great Queer "Yes." We are on the verge of a new affirmation of faith that is just now breaking into voice, symbol, and sign.

I see this in the movement toward LGBTQ inclusion in a growing number of Christian denominations. I feel this in communities of faith taking up the calling to work against LGBTQ bullying and homelessness. I sense this as we work together to craft new liturgies for our shared life: celebrating gender transitions, same-gender weddings, coming out stories, and more. Perhaps most powerfully, I see this affirmation at work in my own family.

Fortunately, our family's story did not end with an exorcism; it was only our beginning. The exorcism allowed us to begin casting out demons of other sorts.

In truth, we learned to say no together to the harmful theologies at work in our lives. It wasn't easy, but it was profoundly healing. We kept talking and learning together even when our theologies, opinions, and core convictions collided.

The horrible thing about grace is that even our enemies get the same kind treatment.

There wasn't a lot of grace in our family when I came out. There wasn't a lot of grace in our family when my brother, my only other sibling, came out a year later (to a similarly warm reception). The church that raised me rejected me. A few months later my brother went through the same judgment and sanction.

Grace's insistence on equal access is hard to come to terms with, but its contagion is awe-inspiring. That's what my family learned. We learned that a little bit of grace was a dangerous thing. It wasn't about convincing my parents in an argument; it wasn't about debating the finer points of Greek or Hebrew translations; and it certainly wasn't about their hermeneutics and exegetical perspectives.

Instead, it was about an exorcism, albeit of a different sort. One where grace came in and threw out our collective games of guilt, retribution, and you'll get what's coming the next time around. That was a beautiful thing to watch.

For our family, it looked like my parents finally forgiving themselves for a lot of things: past marriages, personal shortcomings, their own doubts. For my brother and me, it was learning a radical self-love that allowed us to heal; it was finding a new kind of forgiveness for those who had wounded us even as they tried to love us.

That's the Jesus I found that night, face down in the carpet, amid an exorcism and everything else. A Jesus that showed up with a holy no; ready to move in with grace and new dishes. I believe that our family has continued to meet Jesus along our collective journey. And, together, we have learned to say no and to listen anew.

It hasn't been about being right or winning points in a culture war. For us, it has been about the merciful grace of God that keeps showing up during exorcisms and the most unlikely of places to say, "Enough, drop the stones, there's a better way."

PART 1: REJECTION

Billy Kluttz works as Director of Music at Church of the Pilgrims (PCUSA) in Washington, DC, and as Evening Service Coordinator at Immanuel Presbyterian Church (USA) in McLean, Virginia. He is passionate about creative liturgy and worship, country and bluegrass music, and the role of technology in the emerging church and nonprofit sector.

The Gospel Reconsidered

Marcus Miller

As if coming out wasn't hard enough the first time, I, like so many LGBT+ Christians, had to come out twice. It was the summer before my freshman year of college. I was on my way to the Philippines for a mission trip with my church youth group. During my eleven-hour flight from Minneapolis to Tokyo, I had ample time to muster the courage to tell my friend what was on my mind. I'll call her Beth. Throughout much of the plane ride, I practiced what I would say to her in my head.

"Beth, I think God is calling me to be single." No! That's not direct enough! "Beth, I have something to tell you. I think there's something wrong with me." No, she still won't know what I'm talking about! "Beth, I am gay." No, that implies I'm okay with that. "Beth, I'm struggling with same-sex attraction." Yes! This will best convey my situation.

As we were meandering around in the Tokyo airport, trying to pass the layover time before we embarked on another seven-hour flight to our final destination in Manila, Philippines, I decided to say something.

"Beth, I think God is calling me to be single."

Looking slightly confused, she looked at me and asked, "Why do you say that?" As I fumbled with the words to say, I tried to maintain composure. I stuttered several times, and the words that finally came out of my mouth were, "I haven't met any girls I like." To which Beth replied, "Oh! You just haven't met the right one yet. Don't worry, it's no big deal. I haven't met a guy that I really like either, so you have nothing to worry about."

I remember feeling confused and torn. Since the conversation ended ambiguously, I knew I would have to bring up my struggle with her again another time.

Rewinding a bit, I came to love the Lord during my sophomore year in high school. I will forever be grateful for the Evangelical Free Church I attended for several years. They helped instill in me a deep passion and love for Jesus. It was there I discovered what having a true relationship with God looked like. However, it was also where I was led to believe a nonaffirming theology of marriage every Sunday morning. More specifically, I believed marriage was meant to be solely between one man and one woman. Anything different was going against God's design. Because of my attraction to other men, this belief presented me with a long and painful journey of attempting to reconcile my deep love for Scripture and my sexuality.

Prayers such as, "God, take these feelings away. I know this is wrong, but I can't help being attracted to that guy who attends the youth group. I want to honor you. Change my desires," were said virtually every single night before I went to bed. I hid my struggle from my family and friends for the longest time, thinking it was just a phase and God would "fix me" eventually.

However, during winter break of my freshman year in college, I began to question my church's theology on marriage. By this point, I had come out as "struggling with same-sex attraction" to my closest friends. Some of these friends were in a campus ministry I was involved with at the University of Iowa that year.

My spring semester at Iowa presented me with some of the lowest points in my life. I was still wrestling with what I thought the Bible taught on marriage. I was content with taking time to study Scripture, do research, and examine this topic from many different angles. I was still involved with the campus ministry, which announced toward the middle of the semester they would be accepting applications to be a leader for the following year. I knew right away I wanted to apply—I loved serving in the church and jumped at any opportunity I had to pour into others' lives.

I applied to be a freshman Bible study leader. Shortly after submitting my application, I had an interview with a leader of the campus ministry. My interview went very well. I was offered a leadership position right then and there. After going over the details of what being a freshman Bible study leader would look like, I was asked whether I had any other questions.

I knew I should come forward with where I was and what I was thinking in terms of theology and marriage. I told the interviewer I was wrestling with what I thought the Bible said about LGBT+ topics, and I had been for the past six months or so. I made it clear I had not landed on a conclusion, and I also told them I was gay. I asked the interviewer, "How does this change things, if at all?"

At the time, I was certain my wrestling and uncertainty would not be an issue. After all, my intentions in becoming a Bible study leader were to share God's love with the freshmen I worked with. I did not think complete uniformity over interpretations of Scripture was a requirement for spreading Christ's love. Sadly, they disagreed.

About a week after I had my initial interview, I was invited to speak with the head pastor of the campus ministry. I thought this meeting was going to be about the leadership position, but as I soon realized, I was actually in for quite the lecture. That pastor's crushing and damaging words will forever be ingrained in my mind. I will never forget the line where the head pastor stated, "Marcus, you're putting your view above God's. You're picking and choosing what you want to see from the Bible. Clearly, your identity isn't in Christ." Needless to say, I was denied the leadership position.

Words cannot even remotely come close to expressing how broken I felt. I was an enthusiastic, Jesus-loving student ready to serve the church and point others to Christ at the University of Iowa, and I was rejected by the very organization in which I had found a home. I felt like my intentions and heart were completely misunderstood. I was absolutely devastated to be denied the opportunity to serve and do what I love most. I had many sleepless nights and even thoughts of suicide. I started to believe lies. I reasoned if the nonaffirming theology regarding marriage was correct, then God made a mistake when making me. I became angry at myself and wished I could die.

As I continued to process the meeting I had with the head pastor, I developed a lot of concerns about the way the situation was handled. I was confused; I thought loving Jesus and being willing to serve was ultimately what was most important. Furthermore, I thought this campus ministry would be an excellent place for me to wrestle with a difficult topic. However, instead of being welcomed with open arms, I was presented with a conditional relationship: I had to completely submit to the ministry's theological stances in order for them to accept me. It hurt me because I really wanted to engage in discussion about LGBT+ topics, but I felt silenced and looked down on for wrestling with what they thought the Bible said. This situation planted the seed in my head to question whether the resistance to LGBT+ inclusion was a question of theology, or whether it was a manifestation of the desire to maintain control. To me, if theology was the real concern, it would make more sense for the campus ministry, and other Christian organizations to engage in conversation about LGBT+ topics that included multiple perspectives. Instead, I felt that the church viewed any dissent as a threat to their long-held control.

Despite the pain I experienced during my second semester, I continued to dig into Scripture to look for answers. As I continued to wrestle with my thoughts, I began to make an important distinction: it wasn't God's love for me that wavered, it was the church's. While I cannot recall the specific moment when I changed my mind on what I thought the Bible taught on marriage, I do remember coming out the second time to that same friend, Beth. This time, I was very happy and excited to share who I was and who God made me to be. I came to understand that it is nearly impossible to appreciate your Creator when your theology says you are created to be inherently flawed simply because of sexual orientation. The moment I came to fully embrace myself was the moment I came to fully embrace the fact that I was fearfully and wonderfully made, and that I was made in God's image. The juxtaposition of my two coming out experiences, the former filled with shame and fear and the latter filled with peace and joy, highlights the bad and good fruit that come from having a nonaffirming versus an affirming theology.

I came to realize that when a church preaches a Gospel that mandates the automatic exclusion of LGBT+ people from fully participating in God's kingdom, that church is preaching an incomplete Gospel. God doesn't build walls to prevent people from experiencing Him, He tears walls down. And here's the deal: Jesus has already won the argument as to whether LGBT+ Christians are included in the body of Christ—His death, His resurrection, and His life were for everyone, without exception.

Today, I am a student at the University of Iowa. I am currently in the process of working with a local church, Sanctuary Community Church, to form a campus ministry called Love Works. It is set to be an official student group by the spring semester of 2017. Love Works is a fully inclusive ministry aimed at sharing the good news of Jesus with everyone at the University of Iowa. While the focus is and always will be on Jesus, there will be an emphasis on two major things. First, due to our understanding that God's heart is for the marginalized and that social justice is something God cares deeply about, we will boldly and unapologetically seek to advocate for those whose voices are often overshadowed by those in power, which undoubtedly includes the LGBT+ community. Second, recognizing Jesus' model of serving others, we will seek to serve others in tangible ways through volunteering. (Note the play on words in the name of our organization, Love Works.)

I write this to encourage those who have felt ostracized, those who have not been as fortunate as I have to be able to speak up, and those currently suffering in silence—if God can use me, He can most definitely use you. I once seriously considered suicide. Now, I am about to launch a ministry with the goal of reaching many people who have traditionally been excluded from the church. This isn't on my doing—it's the power of the Gospel.

The thing about Jesus is that everyone is welcome to His table. I am confident that the table will continue to grow as more and more Christians become aware of the damages a nonaffirming theology can inflict on the lives of LGBT+ people. The only direction we have to go is forward. If we rise together as the body of Christ, we can make massive strides toward equality throughout the church and shape it to look more and more like what God's kingdom will look like. The most effective way to realize this is to use your voice in whatever way you can. Whether talking with close friends or publicly and proudly declaring your status as an LGBT+ Christian, I promise you, God can and will use your voice in powerful ways.

Marcus Miller is a student at the University of Iowa, studying political science and ethics & public policy. He plans on attending law school after graduation, with the hopes of using law to advocate for others as either a prosecutor or public defender. In addition to being a student, Marcus is also a Resident Assistant (RA) in a residence hall for first-year students. Whether it be helping residents find various buildings on campus or grieving with residents after their loved ones have passed away, the RA role allows Marcus to do what he loves most—serving others. Marcus would like to thank his family, friends, and spiritual mentors for helping him get to where he is at now.

Dear Church

Brandan Robertson

Dear Church,
 Hello. It's Me.

You know. The heretic. The one who walked away. The backslider. Hello from the other side.

You know. I've loved you for a long time. Ever since I was twelve years old, when I walked down the aisle of the old Baptist church.

I didn't have an ounce of hope in my soul. At the time, I was the son of an abusive alcoholic father. I grew up in a trailer park where a vision for the future wasn't our focus. We were just hoping to get to next week.

At twelve, I was crushed. I had no plans for my life. I felt worthless. But as I made my way down that aisle and fell to my knees at that altar, tears washed down my face as the congregation was singing:

"Just as I am without one plea, but that thy blood was shed for me, and that thou bidst me come to thee, Oh Lamb of God, I come."

I felt a love so powerful, so transformative, so redemptive, from a Heavenly Father who loved me more than my earthly Father ever could. I heard a Gospel that was truly good news for my young soul. I felt, for the first time, the spark of hope. I believed, for the first time, that my life had a purpose, had a meaning.

Dear Church, you have shown me so much love. You've formed me. You've made me into the man I am today.

It was just a few months after that experience with God, I sat in my backyard reading the Bible and I felt a gentle yet powerful tug at my heart. I sensed God calling me. Calling me to be a pastor. To give my life to serve his church. To preach his word. To bring the love and hope that I had found in Jesus to the world around me. And ever since then, that's been the focus of my life.

Dear Church, you taught me so much about what it is to be a follower of Jesus. I've seen your love poured out on me, like the time when dozens of people showed up at our dilapidated trailer unannounced, offering to do renovations, replacing floors, buying groceries, and handing a wad of money to us to help my struggling family get by another week.

I've seen you reach out to people experiencing homelessness. I have seen you advocate on behalf of the voiceless. I have watched you preach the Gospel to the most lost and hopeless individuals, and I have seen new life spring forth because of you.

Dear Church, I've given my life to serve you. From internships, to Bible college and seminary. Every ounce of my energy for the past decade has been given to preparing to teach you, to guide you, to give back to you all that you have given me. I love you and believe in you. I believe you have the power to transform the world.

Dear Church, my heart beats for you.

But something has happened recently and *everything seems to have changed.*

Dear Church, you taught me that I was created in the image and likeness of an eternally expansive, diverse, uncontainable, and indescribable God. Doesn't it make sense, then, that I would be unique, diverse . . . different? Doesn't that mean that we should not be seeking so much uniformity, but instead seeking out uniqueness? So that when we come together as a whole, we make up a big, beautiful, diverse body that mirrors that image of God?

Why then, have you told me that I can no longer truly reflect the image of God because I'm queer? Where has the image of God gone? Isn't it still here? Don't I still bear it? Doesn't God delight in me, just as I am?

Or was that just part of the sales pitch?

Dear Church, why is it that the moment when I feel most truly authentic and most truly connected to God, that you have pushed me away and said I am invalid? Why must who I am as a person cause you to fear me so much? Since when did I become such a problem?

When I kept my sexuality hidden, you lauded me. You told me I was anointed of God. That I was going to be used by God to change the world. Every week after church dozens of older church members would come up to me to tell me that they were so proud of me and knew that God's hand was on my life. Now, when I walk into that same church, I only get side glares and people telling me that they're "praying for me."

What's changed?

That I'm more honest? More authentic? More devoted to Christ than ever before? Yet nothing is the same between us. Instead of a beloved member of your community, *I'm a stranger and exile in the house of God*. The place where I once found a warm embrace has now become a place of rejection and scorn.

Dear Church, you tell me you only do this because you love me. But love doesn't check a persons sexuality or gender identity before embracing them. Yet, you tell me, "This is only for you good" and "I just feel that God wants me to share this with you."

You look at me from across the table, or worse, from behind a computer screen, and lay out a case for just how deceived and dangerous I have become. I've received message after message that say things like, and I quote:

> Certainly you're a leader, Brandan. It is safe to say that in current trajectory of your life you will usher many into a hellish existence. And when you need the blood of Christ to wash away your sins, where will you turn, now that you have renounced His redeeming work so thoroughly. But I already know, you have a victim mentality and you use your sense of victimhood to victimize others. Your behavior is repugnant to me.

Comments like this are not random. They come from former friends, mentors, pastors. Message after message, you shame me. Rebuke me. Condemn me. Without ever actually talking to me. Asking about my life, you assume the worst. You seem no longer to care for me as a person. You only care that I renounce my honesty and return to the shadows of your theological perspective.

No one should have to face such condemnation. Especially from those who bear the name of the Christ who proclaimed, "I have not come to condemn, but to redeem."

Dear Church, much to your surprise, I still have a deep relationship with God. I still read the Bible. I love the Bible. Good grief, I'm even working on a second degree in the Bible and theology.

I know what this book says. I know what God wants for me. And just because we've come to different conclusions about how I live my life and serve our God doesn't mean that I need to be your next evangelistic effort.

There can be space at the table of God's grace for both of us. Christ heals divisions. He calls us to set aside our differences—yes, even differences about what is or is not sin.

Dear Church, don't you believe the words of Scripture?

Don't you believe what the Apostle Paul wrote in the Letter to the Romans?

> Who are you to judge another persons servants? So stop judging each other. Instead, never put a stumbling block or obstacle in the way of your brother or sister. God's kingdom isn't about what one person thinks is unclean and what another thinks isn't, but about righteousness, joy, and peace in the Holy Spirit. So let's strive for the things that bring peace and the things that build each other up.

Dear Church, why have you slammed your door in my face? Will you heed Paul's word?

Dear Church, didn't Jesus say that we shall know true disciples by their fruit? Have you heard these stories? Do you see these lives? We're passionately giving ourselves over to God for the good of our world. Our lives are overflowing with love, and joy, and peace, and patience, and. . . well, you know the list. Why, then, are you so quick to invalidate our salvation?

How could I have been saved so profoundly just one year ago and now be considered unclean? Has the cross of Christ become weakened? Has the power of his resurrection come up deficient?

Dear Church, please explain to me how my sexuality has become a "Gospel" issue. Since when has the announcement of God's kingdom and salvation through Christ ever been based upon what gender somebody falls in love with? Please tell me how disagreement about the interpretation of six verses out of over 30,000 in the Bible have come to represent the "greatest threat to the church" today.

Dear Church, what are you so afraid of? Doesn't the perfect love of Christ cast out all fear? Dear Church, where is your love?

Dear Church, don't you believe in the power of the living and active word of God?

Dear Church, believe it or not, it's not in spite of, but *because* of the Word that I have decided to "come out" as queer. It's precisely because I believe that God is still speaking to us and that the kingdom of Heaven is in our midst that I fight for the rights of my LGBT+ siblings in society and in the church.

Dear Church, we're not an issue. We're not imaginary. We are queer followers of Jesus and we are *here*. We have a voice. We are committed to the radical, self-sacrificial way of Jesus, our Lord. And while I know that our existence doesn't fit in your theological paradigm, *it is reality*. And when reality and theology clash, *it's probably time to rethink your theology*. When your theology pushes people away from God, from hope, from life. Something has gone terribly wrong. When shame, self hatred, and fear is the result of your teaching, you can be assured that your words are not from God.

Dear Church, even in the midst of all of this, I still have grace for you. God has chosen to make up his kingdom of beautifully broken people among whom I am the chief. I know that many of you have the best intentions. You really do want to do what's right. To stand on the truth. To love me in the way that you believe that God demands. I have been sitting in your seat. I too struggled to accept LGBT+ people. To accept myself. I understand your struggle. I've been there too. It took a lot of work. A lot of time. A lot of prayer. A lot of openness to the Holy Spirit to stand where I am today.

And that's all I am asking of you today.

Not to change your mind overnight. But to be humble. Make room in your life to learn. To rethink. To ask hard questions. To listen to and accept the stories that make you feel uncomfortable. Do it, not because your life needs to center around this topic, but because of the fact that there *are* people in your life, in your faith community, that are LGBT+. I guarantee it. Do it because Christ commands it of you. Do it because *every person matters to God*. Do it because *real* lives are on the line. Do it because the Gospel of Jesus calls us to sacrifice our comfort, our privilege, and our power for the good of the other. The least of these. The minority.

In that way, I guess, this is, in fact, a Gospel issue.

Because if the Gospel you proclaim isn't good news to the poor, liberation to the captive, recovery of sight to the blind, and God's ridiculous grace *for all*, then it isn't the Gospel of Jesus. It's, by definition, a false Gospel.

This kingdom is a kingdom for misfits. For minorities. For queers. For outcasts. For those who don't seem to belong. This kingdom is a kingdom for all who reflect the image and likeness of God. And I've got news for you. That means *all of us*.

Dear Church, LGBT+ people *are already* the church. You don't have the power to exclude us from participating in Christ. The table, the kingdom, and the power is God's and God's alone. And he has welcomed us in.

Dear Church, God is doing a new thing in our day. God is decentralizing those who have held power and privilege in his name for too long. A revival is breaking forth. Droves are finding renewed life in the way of Christ. Our voice is getting louder. Our influence is gaining strength. And our agenda, well, it's simple:

To see the kingdom of this world transformed into the kingdom of our Lord and of his Christ.

To see justice roll forth like a river. Equity and peace on every corner of the earth. It's to embody the Spirit of Christ to our world.

And that's a dangerous agenda, indeed. For it challenges the systems of power and oppression in our world. It threatens to unhinge all that we've built to make our lives comfortable. But it's an unstoppable one.

And to my LGBT+ siblings, let me say it again. We are already the church. We don't need to wait to be included. We already are. Just as we are.

We *are* the body of Christ.

We *are* included in the kingdom of God.

We *do* bear the image and likeness of God.

We are *not* broken.

We must stand strong, live into our calling to be ambassadors of Christ and his reconciling message to our world. We must refuse to return evil for evil, judgment for judgment. We must embody grace, patience, and forgiveness. But that doesn't mean we stay silent.

We must open our mouths. Open our hearts. Open our lives. And let the light of Christ within us shine forth, so that the world can see our good works and glorify God because of us. We are the channels of renewal and revival. We are the future.

May we not grow proud or resentful. May we instead seek to embody both grace and truth. Because truth will win out. Grace will win out. Love will win out in the end. I guarantee it.

Dear Church, Here we are. *This is our witness.*

Brandan Robertson is the author of *Nomad: A Spirituality For Travelling Light* (2016) and writes regularly for *Patheos* and *The Huffington Post*. He is the founder and executive director of Nomad Partnerships, a nonprofit working to foster spiritual and social evolution around the world. He served as the immediate past national spokesperson of Evangelicals for

Marriage Equality and has served on the U.S. State Department's Working Group on Religion and LGBT+ Rights and the Democratic National Convention's LGBT+ Advisory Board. Brandan earned his Bachelor in Pastoral Ministry & Theology from Moody Bible Institute and his Master of Theological Studies from Iliff School of Theology.

PART 2

RECONCILIATION

For many LGBT+ Christians, the process of reconciling their faith and their sexuality is a long and strenuous process, but when it finally clicks, there is a sense of sheer liberation experienced as we step into our God-created identity, fully knowing that we are loved and celebrated by God. In my own journey to reconcile my faith and sexuality, I didn't find the path forward through wrestling with the familiar "clobber passages" in the Scriptures, but rather through discovering a trajectory toward greater inclusion in the Scriptures, which I came to discover is the heart of the Gospel. To begin this section, I want to pause momentarily from sharing stories of LGBT+ Christians and briefly lay out the theological case for inclusion that led me to fully embrace my God-given identity and enabled me to see the powerful work of God's Spirit through the witness of LGBT Christians.

The foundational beliefs of the Christian faith are often summarized in what the writers of the New Testament call "the Gospel." This word Gospel comes from the Greek εὐαγγέλιον (euangelion), which literally means "to bring good news." This word "gospel" appears dozens of times throughout the New Testament, and is used to refer to the message that Jesus himself came to proclaim and embody, containing the keys to salvation for humankind. To begin thinking about the metanarrative of Christian theology, there is no more essential place to start than here. Throughout the biblical texts themselves and Christian theology through the ages, there is much variance in what exactly the message of the Gospel is. For our purposes, I will root my understanding in the definition that the writer of the Gospel of Mark has Jesus speaking, because many biblical scholars agree that Mark's Gospel contains some of the most reliable quotes from Jesus, based on earlier source texts.[1] In chapter 1 of the Gospel, the author of Mark says:

> Jesus came into Galilee announcing God's good news, saying: "Now is the time! Here comes God's kingdom! Change your hearts and lives, and trust this good news!"[2]

According to this passage, the "good news" that Jesus preached was quite concise and simple: It is the announcement that the kingdom of God was coming and an invitation to change our hearts and lives to trust in the emerging reality of that kingdom. Throughout the rest of Jesus' teachings, as portrayed in the synoptic Gospels, he repeats this message about the arrival of the kingdom of God over and over again. The gospel according to Jesus is about this new reality he called the kingdom of God, and therefore, this must be the foundation of all Christian theology and practice.

What, then, is the kingdom of God, and what impact might it have on our understanding of the inclusion of sexual and gender minorities in the life of the church? To answer this question, we turn to the words of the Apostle Paul in his Epistle to the Romans where Paul writes, "For the kingdom of God is . . . justice, and peace, and joy in the Holy Spirit."[3] In this statement, Paul, writing to the Church at Rome in the midst of great conflict over how to observe Jewish laws and customs, suggests that the kingdom of God is not some far-off, supernatural reality, but rather a Spirit-led movement of justice, peace, and joy, realities that should be experienced in the life of the church and in the world here and now.

Theologian Jürgen Moltmann builds on Paul's definition, suggesting that the kingdom of God is a present, tangible reality, brought and demonstrated in the person of Jesus himself, as well as a spiritual reality, described as an ever-deepening union with God. Moltmann writes:

> [The] Kingdom of God—that means God is near and present and allows God's creatures to participate in God's attributes, in God's

---

1. For more on the Marcan Priority theory, see Mark Goodacre, *The Synoptic Problem: A Way Through the Maze* (London: T & T Clark, 2001) 20–23.

2. Mark 1:14–15, CEB.

3. Rom 14:17.

glory and beauty, in God's vivacity and God's goodness, because at the same time God participates in the attributes of God's creatures, in their finiteness, in their vulnerability, and in their morality (1 John 4:6). . . .The Church is not there for it's own sake but rather for the "concern of Jesus." All inherent interest of the Church itself . . . must be subordinated to the interests of the Kingdom of God. . . . The divine mission of the Church consists [of] bringing the oppressed their freedom, the humiliated their human dignity, and those without rights their rights. . . . [We must] participate in the Kingdom of God and today let something from the rebirth of all things become visible which Christ will complete on his day.[4]

Moltmann, echoing the words of both Paul and Jesus, furthers our understanding that the kingdom of God must be understood to be a present and growing reality of union with God, resulting in the expansion of justice, peace, and equity for all of God's creatures. According to Jesus, in his many parables about the kingdom of God, it is both a present reality and one that continues to grow and progress. When Jesus speaks of the kingdom, he likens it to leaven in dough[5] and a mustard seed planted in a field.[6] The imagery used here is one of gradual growth and expansion, requiring human effort to knead the dough and cultivate the seeds that are planted. Another way to understand this is that Jesus, in his life, planted the seeds of the kingdom. He demonstrated in his own actions what it looks like to live in step with the kingdom of God, or the world as God intends it to be. He then left it up to his disciples to cultivate the seeds so that the kingdom of God would grow and expand throughout the earth as the reality of justice and equity for all people.

To be a disciple of Jesus is to be one who "changes your heart and life and trusts" in the path that Jesus demonstrated.[7] According to the teachings of the Gospels, this is what will bring ultimate wholeness to our world. But as we clearly see throughout the entire life of Jesus, his path is not an easy or convenient one to follow. It requires humility, sacrifice, and selflessness. It shouldn't be surprising to us, then, that a majority of what is sold as "Christianity" in our world has little to do with this message of liberation and equality for all people, but instead has been abstracted by theological mus-

4. Jürgen Moltmann, "Jesus and the Kingdom of God," *The Asbury Theological Journal* 48 (Spring 1993) 5–18.

5. Matt 13:33.

6. Matt 13:31–32.

7. Mark 1:15.

ings and understood to be about a supernatural salvation in the afterlife, with little influence on the world we live in now.

If the message at the heart of Christianity is a message of an ever-expanding reality of justice and equality for societies most marginalized and oppressed, then that must be the starting point for any conversation pertaining to inclusion in the church. As prominent black liberation theologian James Cone notes:

> Any view of the gospel that fails to understand the Church as that community whose work and consciousness are defined by the community of the oppressed is not Christian and is thus heretical.[8]

In Cone's understanding, unless the message that is preached and embodied by Christian communities fully reflects the life and teaching of Jesus and his preferential option for the poor, marginalized, and oppressed of society, then it cannot be accepted as true Christianity.

This understanding of the Gospel has roots in the teachings of Jesus himself and has been a common understanding throughout Christian history. From the early patristic writings[9] through the abolitionist movements of the 1700s,[10] the liberationist movement of the early 1900s,[11] and the feminist movements of the mid-1900s,[12] the idea that the message of Jesus was directed to society's most oppressed groups has undergirded Christian teaching for two thousand years. Any understanding of Christianity that lacks this liberationist undergirding, then, is failing to interpret the Gospel through the lens of Jesus and the writings of the Gospels that cast Christ's entire mission and ministry in a liberationist light.

One major reoccurring theme in the Synoptic Gospels is that Jesus continually finds himself battling with the religious leaders of his day over his seeming disregard for the religious dogma derived from the Hebrew Bible. Over a dozen times throughout the written accounts the Pharisees and Sadducees are found confronting Jesus for his blatant disregard for

---

8. James Cone, *God of the Oppressed* (New York: Orbis, 2000) 37.

9. J. Kameron Carter draws extensively on early Christians sources for liberation in his groundbreaking book, *Race: A Theological Account* (Oxford: Oxford University Press, 2008).

10. See the writings of William Wilberforce.

11. See the work of Gustavo Gutierrez, Jon Sobrino, and James Cone.

12. See the work of Marie Maugeret, Elisabeth Schussler Fiorenza, and Catherine Keller.

biblical law or religious custom.[13] Jesus, however, seems to take great delight in frustrating these religious leaders, offering new interpretations and further progressions on the laws of old. For instance, the Gospel of Matthew records a long series of teachings in which Jesus directly quotes from the Old Testament and then directly contradicts the commandment and raises the ethical standard. He begins his teaching by saying, "Do not think that I have come to abolish the Law, but to fulfill it."[14] The word πληρῶσαι (plērōsai), which is translated "fulfill" in many Bible translations of this verse, can also be translated as "complete." I believe that this translation helps us understand what Jesus is trying to communicate in this teaching.

Progressive revelation is the belief that God reveals more and more truth over time, as humanity is able to receive and adopt the "fullness of truth." In the Christian tradition, Jesus is understood to be the embodiment of the fullness of truth, the example of what a life lived in accordance with the will of God looks like. As the writer of the Epistle to the Hebrews says, "In the past, God spoke through the prophets to our ancestors in many times and many ways. In these final days, though, he has spoken to us through his Son."[15] Jesus is seen as the supreme revelation of God to earth, in whom "the fullness of God was pleased to dwell."[16] His words, then, are seen to be the completion and the truest embodiment of many of the Hebrew Bible's commands, which were only partially or incompletely revealed.

In Matt 5, we witness Jesus building upon laws from the Hebrew Bible and bringing them to a more complete and holistic ethical standard. For instance, he says:

> You have heard that it was said, "An eye for an eye and a tooth for a tooth." But I say to you that you must not oppose those who hurt you. If people slap you on your right cheek, you must turn the left cheek to them as well.[17]

Jesus quotes directly from Exod 21:24, and then significantly amends the commandment, raising the ethical standard. Now, his disciples aren't permitted to retaliate, but are commanded to embrace nonviolent resistance as the norm. The ethic has been altered, the standard has been raised.

13. For a sampling of these confrontations, see Matt 15:1; 16:1–6; 23:1–4; Luke 11:37; 14:3.

14. Matt 5:17.

15. Heb 1:1–2.

16. Col 1:19.

17. Matt 5:38–39.

Jesus renders the old law irrelevant in light of his new law, rooted in unconditional love. Jesus does this six times over the course of Matt 5, each
time taking a biblical commandment and amending it to be more ethical
and just.

Jesus clearly has no problem amending Scripture. He clearly is not
working from a paradigm of biblical inerrancy. For Jesus, the Bible is a living text, always evolving and always being brought nearer to "completion."
This makes sense when one realizes that even the rabbis of old viewed the
Scriptures as texts to be reinterpreted, revised, and reconfigured based on
the current era and context that they found themselves in. This tradition
was know as midrash, which is described by Hebrew literature scholar David Stern in the following way:

> [Midrash is] a specific name for the activity of biblical interpreta-
> tion as practiced by the Rabbis of the land of Israel in the first five
> centuries of the common era. . . . By the end of the biblical period,
> the locus for [the search for God's will] appears to have settled on
> the text of the Torah where, it was now believed, God's will for the
> present moment was to be found.[18]

In other words, midrash was a traditional rabbinical method, which
relied upon the written text of the Torah to find wisdom and guidance for
the present moment. This resulted in texts being taken out of their original
context (*the* chief sin among evangelical theologians) and applied to situations in which the original author would never have even considered. But
this was how Scripture was to be used, as a channel through which the
Spirit of God could illumine old wisdom for new circumstance, resulting in
new interpretations, new ideas, and even new additions to and subtractions
from the biblical text. A few centuries after the initial writing of the Torah,
the rabbis were already reinterpreting some of the strict commands of the
Torah in order to make life more reasonable and practical for the average
Jewish person. Throughout history, the biblical texts were seen as "living
and active"[19] and not static and unchanging. This is how Jesus viewed the
texts himself, bringing many of the existing ethical interpretations of laws
from the Hebrew Bible to their completion through consideration of those
on the margins. To many, this looked like transgression of the law, and indeed, it was. But in transgressing one version of the law, Jesus revealed a

18. Adele Berlin and David Stern, *Jewish Study Bible* (Oxford: Oxford University
Press, 2004) 1864.

19. Heb 4:12.

higher standard for his disciples to live by. Biblical scholar Cheryl Anderson notes that

> Jesus violated [traditional] standards to reincorporate those who had been excluded. . . . The inclusive table fellowship of Jesus stands in stark contrast to the exclusive table fellowship of the Pharisees.[20]

Furthermore, Jesus makes it clear that God's revelatory work will not cease with him. Indeed, he tells his disciples that the Holy Spirit would continue her revelatory work indefinitely. Jesus says to his disciples, "I still have much to tell you, but you cannot yet bear to hear it. However, when the Spirit of truth comes, [it] will guide you into all the truth."[21] In other words, as Jesus is looking toward his nearing death, he tells the disciples that there is much more he desires for them to know, but doesn't believe they are able to bear it at the present time. This is a fundamental Christian belief—that God has (and will) reveal truth progressively, over time, as humanity is able to "bear" or comprehend it. As reformed evangelical theologian Vern Poythress writes, describing progressive revelation:

> God did not say everything at once. The earlier communications take into account the limitations in the understanding of people at earlier times. The later communications build on the earlier.[22]

God is still speaking. Though the biblical canon may be closed as a matter of tradition, the ongoing revelatory work of God clearly continues to unfold throughout human history, leading society toward higher ethical ideals of inclusion, equality, and wholeness. This reality has been and is currently experienced by followers of Christ throughout the ages and is completely aligned with the teachings and expectations of Jesus. If we are to be faithful to God in our present age, we must pay close attention to the nudges of the Spirit, gently calling us to step beyond our beliefs and traditions to widen the gates of the kingdom of God.

20. Cheryl Anderson, *Ancient Laws and Contemporary Controversies: The Need for Inclusive Biblical Interpretation* (Oxford: Oxford University Press, 2009) 92.

21. John 16:12–13.

22. Peter Lillback et al., *Seeing Christ in All of Scripture: Hermeneutics at Westminster Theological Seminary* (Philadelphia: Westminster Seminary, 2016) 10.

PART 2: RECONCILIATION

Reexamining Biblical Texts: Exploring Inclusive Biblical Interpretation

When one examines the way that Jesus and the early apostles used Scripture, we begin to see a clear trajectory toward higher ethical standards and a more inclusive vision for the kingdom of God. In 2001, evangelical theologian William Webb published a groundbreaking book where he posited a hermeneutical lens for interpreting Scripture that he called "the redemptive-movement hermeneutic."[23] This hermeneutic traced the redemptive trajectory of ethics from the Hebrew Bible to the New Testament, showing that ethical consciousness of society continually grew, albeit slowly, toward a more inclusive and equal posture for all people. Webb's hermeneutic argued that faithful Christians are called to move beyond the static words of Scripture, taking the "spirit" of the words and applying them to our modern contexts to help us determine the faithful response to our ethical questions. Webb writes:

> Scripture does not present a "finalized ethic" in every area of human relationship. . . . To stop where the Bible stops (with its isolated words) ultimately fails to reapply the redemptive spirit of the text as it spoke to the original audience. It fails to see that further reformation is possible. . . .While Scripture had a positive influence in its time, we should take that redemptive spirit and move to an even better, more fully realized ethic today.[24]

Webb's argument opens the door for continued societal reform, based on the spirit of the biblical texts, rather than the static words themselves. And while Webb's "redemptive-movement hermeneutic" was groundbreaking for the evangelical world in 2001, it is hardly a new idea or concept. Instead, it has been clearly demonstrated in the field of biblical interpretation[25] and in the texts themselves for thousands of years. As we noted earlier, feminist and liberationist theologians have relied on ethical trajectories in Scripture and the cultural context of the writer as the interpretive key to unlock the liberating power of the biblical text. Feminist theologian Carol Lakey Hess notes:

23. William Webb, *Slaves, Women & Homosexuals: Exploring the Hermeneutics of Cultural Analysis* (Downers Grove, IL: InterVarsity, 2001).

24. Ibid., 247.

25. Similar theological arguments have been made by a wide array of theologians in the modern era such as J. R. Daniel Kirk, Megan DeFranza, Dale Martin, and I. Howard Marshall.

> [Biblical] texts . . . reflect the prevailing cultural ethos. . . . We must
> use these to recognize that the biblical writers were human per-
> sons immersed in—though not limited to—the language, mores,
> customs, and assumptions of their day. . . . Some texts both reflect
> and challenge the cultural assumptions. . . . By looking at what is
> new, rather than what is the same, sometimes we can see a trajec-
> tory towards greater liberation.[26]

Here, Hess reflects the hermeneutical idea of a redemptive ethical trajectory that has been demonstrated throughout biblical interpretation for
thousands of years. As theologian Derek Flood echoes:

> The New Testament is not a final unchangeable eternal ethic, but
> rather the "first major concrete steps" from the dominant reli-
> gious and political narrative . . . towards a better way rooted in
> compassion.[27]

One biblical text where this redemptive trajectory is most clearly on
display is in the Book of Acts chapter 10, where the Apostle Peter falls into
a God-induced trance and is called to preach the Gospel to the unclean
Gentiles for the first time. In this account, Peter sees a vision of a sheet
coming out of heaven, holding a plethora of biblically "unclean" animals.
As Peter observes the sheet with confusion, he hears the voice of God speak
to him three times, saying, "Rise up, kill, and eat." Peter, being a faithful
Jew and student of Scripture, argues with the voice of God, saying that he
could not kill and eat these unclean animals because to do so would be a
violation of Scripture. On the third go around, the voice of God responds to
Peter saying, "Do not call unclean that which I have made clean." With that,
Peter awakens from the trance and finds the servant of Cornelius, a Roman
Centurion, knocking on his door, requesting that he come and speak to
Cornelius and his household about the Gospel. Immediately, Peter realizes
that this vision was not about unclean foods but unclean people, the Gentiles. Peter reluctantly goes with the servants to Cornelius' house to preach
the Gospel to them. As Peter arrives, he says to Cornelius, "You yourselves
know that it is unlawful for a Jew to associate with or to visit a Gentile; but

---

26. Carol Lakey Hess, *Caretakers of Our Common House: Women's Development in
Communities of Faith* (Nashville: Abingdon, 1997) 197–98.

27. Derek Flood, *Disarming Scripture: Cherry-Picking Liberals, Violence-Loving Con-
servatives, and Why We All Need to Learn to Read the Bible like Jesus Did* (San Francisco:
Metanoia, 2014) 127.

God has shown me that I should not call anyone profane or unclean."[28] As Peter preaches, we are told, "while Peter was still speaking, the Holy Spirit fell upon all who heard the word."[29] The Spirit falls upon the Gentiles, an example of the Spirit of God doing something that was previously understood to be immoral or unbiblical.

Peter's actions of entering a Gentile's home and baptizing them into the church was seen by the apostles and elders in Jerusalem to be a grave violation of biblical law. After hearing about Peter's actions, he was summoned to meet with the council who proceeded to "criticize him for this apparent sin.[30] Peter then recounts the entire situation, from his vision to the baptism of Cornelius' house, and concludes, "If then God gave them the same gift that he gave us when we believed in the Lord Jesus Christ, who was I that I could hinder God?"[31] When the Apostolic Council heard this, we are told, "They praised God, saying, "Then God has given even to the Gentiles the repentance that leads to life."[32] Both Peter and the council are open and willing to change their long-held theological beliefs and practices to coincide with the experiential evidence of God's Spirit working among the Gentiles. For these leaders, there is no deep biblical deliberation, but an acknowledgement that if God so desired to save the Gentiles, then the apostles' only job was to celebrate and welcome the new thing that God was doing in their midst.

For decades, this story of the conversion of the Gentiles has been a cornerstone for inclusive theology, demonstrating both the redemptive trajectory of Scripture and the value of experience and testing the fruits. As queer theologian Patrick Cheng notes, the dissolution of clean and unclean religious categories began to dissolve in the life and ministry of Jesus himself, in the ways that he interacted with and included some of the most "unholy" individuals in Jewish theological consciousness, and this trend clearly continues in the theological approach of the earliest apostles.[33] Therefore, it can be logically deduced that when we observe the approach of Peter and the apostles in regards to the authority given to ongoing the

28. Acts 10:28.
29. Acts 10:44.
30. Acts 11:2.
31. Acts 11:17.
32. Acts 11:18.
33. Patrick Cheng, *Radical Love: An Introduction to Queer Theology* (New York: Seabury, 2011) 80.

revelatory work of the Holy Spirit and the role of experience, we see a regular pattern of theological growth and evolution toward greater inclusivity. Cheryl Anderson writes:

> Biblical scholars are now advancing understandings of God and interpretations of the biblical text that are different from traditional ones. Yet they are different only because they reflect the political and economic realities of women, the poor, and the foreigner and consider the impact that traditional interpretations have on these groups. Although those who uphold the traditional Christian interpretations, today's Pharisees, vilify this contextual approach, it is exactly the kind of approach that Jesus used.[34]

In our contemporary era, it seems clear that the Spirit of God continues to call humanity forward toward the higher ethical standards, and this belief is accepted by a majority of contemporary progressive Christians when they examine their theological and ethical beliefs about slavery, the treatment of women, the discipline of children, divorce, corporal punishment, and a wide array of other ethical issues in which modern Christian teaching is significantly more ethical than what is prescribed in the Scriptures. Webb goes to great lengths to demonstrate that while the New Testament is, for instance, the final revelation of Scripture, the ethical perspectives of the New Testament have by no means been taken to their fullest realization in the static words of Scripture itself.[35] As one explores how the abolitionists, for example, viewed the trajectory of Scripture, it becomes abundantly clear that it was their understanding of the spirit of the biblical texts, rather than the plain, literal reading of the text, that directed their theological fight to end slavery in the United States and was a source of great critique from traditionalist, pro-slavery Christians.[36] The same approach must be faithfully applied as Christians grapple with the "clobber passages" that seem to condemn same-sex relationships.

It can be argued that throughout the entire biblical canon, there is a trajectory that shows how the biblical authors' understanding of gender roles and sex evolved throughout time toward a more egalitarian approach. While examples of ethical regression are also present in the New

---

34. Anderson, *Ancient Laws and Contemporary Controversies*, 87.

35. William Webb, "The Limits of a Redemptive-Movement Hermeneutic: A Focused Response to T. R. Schreiner," *Evangelical Quarterly* 74 (2003) 330.

36. Mark Noll, *The Civil War as a Theological Crisis* (Chapel Hill: University of North Carolina Press, 2015).

Testament—for instance, when one looks at how Paul in various contexts amplifies his belief that women should be silent and submissive in church— by and large the direction of the ethical trajectories in the Bible point toward a more liberating and inclusive posture. It is in these same trajectories that the keys for full inclusion for LGBT+ people into the life of the church can be found. As New Testament scholar J. R. Daniel Kirk notes:

> For the same reason that we cannot claim anymore that men are better than women, for the same reason that we do not hold to a biblical view of marriage in which a man owns his wife, for the same reason that we err in excluding women from leading as they are gifted by the Spirit, the ground has been cut out from the ancient framework that excluded the notion of same-sex intercourse.[37]

The ethical trajectories of the biblical texts generally point toward more inclusive ways of seeing and being in the world. And as we will see in the next section of this book, there is much evidence to suggest that the Holy Spirit is working in and through sexual and gender minorities to bring about redemption and renewal in contemporary Christianity. It is this combination of biblical ethical trajectories and experience that should lead contemporary Christians on the same theological journey of Peter and the earliest apostles. If the Spirit of God moves among LGBT+ people, who are Christians to stand in the way of the work of God? One can almost hear the Spirit speaking to the church today saying, "Do not call unclean that which I have made clean!" once again.[38]

In this section, we will hear stories of how LGBT+ Christians reconciled their faith and sexuality and boldly stepped into their place at the table of God's grace. Like Peter's account to the council of apostles, as you read these stories, I am confident that you will sense the powerful movement of God's Spirit in and through these queer lives and see the evident trajectory of the kingdom in each story.

37. J. R. Daniel Kirk, "Trajectories Toward Gay Inclusion?" *Storied Theology* (February 27, 2016) http://www.patheos.com/blogs/storiedtheology/2016/02/27/trajectories-toward -gay-inclusion/.

38. Acts 10:15.

The Bridges We Walk

Lauren Ileana Sotolongo

Part I

I am the third of four siblings. I was the first to "go away" to college (living forty minutes away from my parent's house). My parents and grandparents were Cuban refugees. The foundation of our family is firm—set and dried in cement.

I am a crack in the cement.

I have been trying to reconcile two halves of my soul for years. Six months after moving to Washington DC, the two halves met. The tension built until—after coffee with a friend—everything burst. The Physical embodiment of self spoke to the Christian expression of self. Each said the same thing. *It's nice to finally meet you, but I don't think it's safe here.*

What I would call "The Spirit" spoke something different to both parts. It said: *You are a whole "one," not a disjointed "many." This weight isn't holy; these chains are not Mine. It is time.*

I called my mom that night, and we cried. I then told the rest of my family—or they found out—slowly.

My foundation is an ocean, constantly flowing; my family's is sturdy, cemented in love. I am learning that no one can be "home," when your own bones are hostile territory.

I am a crack in the cement. But I am learning to call the tearing of certain veils "holy."

I am a crack in the cement. But I think light is pushing through.

I think, even in this break, something is growing.

Part II

People got shot in a nightclub and I felt like a body on the floor. And the thing about grief is, it cannot bear any form of "loving challenge." Grief only knows love, or lack of love. Grief only knows an open or shut door.

After the shooting—plastered across news screens, and in the midst of our own Capital Pride in DC—I shared my grief in various social media posts.

My younger brother sent a text on a Wednesday night.

It read, "You okay?"

"I don't know," I said.

I explained briefly; it felt so personal, and heavy. People died at a nightclub. And that same night, I was out, celebrating Pride, at a nightclub. Latino people were killed. I am a Cuban American, and my parents were refugees. I did not know how to justify my pain; only that it was intimate and deep and there.

My younger brother's response to the rocks on my chest; to the rocks in my throat; to the rocks in the thousands of miles that separated our eyes; was: "Aight. Love you punk."

And it was enough. My younger brother is not afraid of crossing lines; I think he is afraid of leaving someone isolated, behind lines that others won't cross. He is less worried about what his love for me means; he is more worried about not giving it.

So he gives.

And it is enough.

Part III

My father's eyelids are heavy. Something in him seems to be drowning, but his eyes are still like autumn-leaves. As a I child, I never looked too closely, but now I do; he is hazelnut coffee with cream (though he always takes his coffee black, no cream—with plenty of sugar).

My father hunts; plays poker; loves quietly; gardens consistently; breaks, builds, remodels, and fixes. He bought me my first knife at age 9. When I was younger, we used to peruse Best Buy excitedly. Home Depot, too. He would say Home Depot was "Disneyland"; Home Depot was the place we went to fix things.

I think my father's veins are splitting, because he does not know how to fix me.

My father has a daughter who may one day bring home a woman and call her "love." The wooden church pews and plastic Sunday chairs we've shared for years tell my father that they can no longer hold me. He hears the echo of questions never asked, because answers spoke clearly; Romans, Soddom, Adam and Eve.

My father is a good man. He also cannot picture a wedding day for a daughter that does not include a man; one who can protect me and lead me to a good God. He cannot picture a wedding day with a woman as the fulfillment of his dreams for me; he cannot picture a wedding day, with a woman by my side; a women who could protect and lead me to a good God.

My father and I cannot adventure through Home Depot to fix me. And I don't think my father wants this. Perhaps that makes him sad too.

He is still the sunrise to me. His eyes, autumn leaves; hazelnut coffee. He tells me stories of Cuba; of running through sugar cane fields near the railroad tracks in a run-down town. He is the sunrise to me. I want to rise with him. I wonder if—one day—he will let me.

I think he loves me just as I am.

My father's eyelids are heavy, but his eyes still shine.

My father's religion is his everything.

But—I think—so am I.

———

Part IV

My mother is a committed teacher. Her favorite subjects are history and forgiveness. She cherishes those lessons etched into the bones and forgotten homes of ancient people; her middle schoolers call her strict—I call her committed to the most beautiful and excellent of things.

Most weeks, I remember the lessons my mother taught me. [How to make *cafe Cubano*; entertain company; shave my legs; order pizza without fear of strangers.]

My mother is a holy rhythm I neglect. Most weeks, I dial her number like a forgotten journal entry. Her smile's soft edges (and warm eyes) are painted across my face like an echo. I carry these echoes like divine prophesy. It is the same way my brave, warrior mother used to carry me in her belly. I think, sometimes, she still tries to carry me.

Some weeks, our words share the pleasantries of afternoon tea; other weeks, they stumble into one another clumsily, like rubbing alcohol against bloody veins. There will always be things that sting, but I will choose to live in uncomfortable proximity to these things; after all, she is my veins. After all, she is this blood.

I have been entrusted to wear her smile the way I used to wear my skinned knees—proud, and rebellious, and slightly challenging the status quo.

I have been taught these things. After all, I am the daughter of a brave, warrior mother.

Most weeks, I remember that her veins are my veins, and her blood rushes through me.

Most weeks, I remember the lessons she taught me.

―――

Part V

I babysat Nephew and Niece while Sister and Brother-In-Law visited wineries.

We rented an AirBnB in Paso Robles, California, and while the "adults" left for the day, me and the kids watched Little Mermaid and sang. My nephew calls me "Tia," and I feel there is no better title in the world.

My sister loves deeply and cries like me. We set up our walls differently (the ones inside our hearts), but it does not mean we don't understand the substance of each other's beings.

She loves me.

They all do.

When I told her about my then-girlfriend, we were in her living room with a rare moment alone, together; she replied, "Lauren, you know what I think." We usually leave things here, because we'll both cry—and have many times.

We love deeply.

They all do.

On this day, though, she returned from the winery, blustery and bright-eyed with my huggable brother-in-law. She rambled quickly about the wines; the beauty of the vineyards; the scenery and the town. She re-counted it like a 7 year old after a field trip. I recounted my trip to the park, with my tiny nephew and niece similarly, mainly because it truly felt like an attempt to summit Everest (which is what having two tiny humans in your care feels like).

She laughed at my recounting. Her eyes flashed, as if to remember something; she took a moment and added—"Oh. And there was this cute guy working at the winery. I would've given him your number but didn't. . .since you're not into dudes."

My heart stopped.

It was the closest we'd gotten to talking positively (or neutrally) about sexuality. No fight; just a simple joke. It was an open-air acknowledgment. Simple; easily missed; wildly important to me; perhaps a misunderstanding. But I do not regret misunderstanding, if I did, because this misunderstanding spelled out "I love you." I will take this as its meaning.

Because she loves me.

Because they all do.

———

Part VI

We mostly avoid eye contact when I visit. He gives a firm hug when I arrive, and a kiss on the cheek. He does the same when I leave.

I think he is acknowledging that he is losing—or has lost—something. I am his little sister. I love his two sons more than I could ever explain. His wife shines like a sunrise and cares a lot too.

It is hard to step in the fire without knowing how—or if—you'll make it out the other side. I think we're all learning the depth of this burning in my family. But Love isn't easily killed; burned at the stake; sacrificed like a body in the street, slain. Love is tougher than gold; refined and reborn like a phoenix; resurrected and remade.

My older brother follows reason like a compass—it is the arrow stuck in his heart. But love isn't easily killed. He hugs me firmly when I come home, and he kisses me on the cheek; he does the same when I leave.

I am learning to call the simplest of things "loving." I am learning to hold closely, the glimpses of something more; words that none of us are ready to speak.

Let's start with a firm hug, and kiss on the cheek.

Part V

I am a crack in the cement.

My hands are shaking, stretched until the muscles tear. My lips are cracking, my skin is cut, and blood is seeping through. But I will stop putting these red stains across manmade letters.

I will love to the bottom of a grave dug for me. I will love to the edges of heaven; I will love to the pit of my stomach and the pit of my limits. I will stop burning my heart with the rams of Ancient Israel. I will remember that I claim to have found a savior.

I will call you my Family. I will try not to burn us, in fearful sacrifice, when I get scared. I hope you will try too.

I am a crack in the cement. But I will not stop loving you.

I hope this isn't a sin too.

Lauren Ileana Sotolongo grew up in a family of Cuban immigrants, who established themselves as educators, public service professionals, and active church leaders in Southern California. With a familial passion for public service instilled at a young age, she found the intersection of her own passions within faith, social justice, and writing. She currently resides in Washington DC, is a proud Tía to four bright-eyed revolutionaries, and can usually be found brewing coffee at a local roastery, or eating Oreos. Her favorite colors are orange and purple.

Before I Pop the Question

Claire Jones

It is a wise move, so anyone with experience will say, before you commit to spend your life in faithful relationship with another person, to make sure you're really sure. It's not a commitment to be entered into lightly or on the spur of the moment, but wholeheartedly and responsibly, before God.

So it came to be that this modest diamond ring I'd bought with flushed cheeks and a pounding heart still sat in its box a month later, in a creaky wooden drawer next to the creaky wooden bed in an otherwise bare cell. I was on a weeklong silent retreat in an ancient monastery tucked many miles out of sight of the hustle and bustle of city life. These were the silent hours in which I would listen to God harder than I'd ever listened before to make absolutely sure this was the right decision to make.

It wasn't my choice of person that I needed to *umm* and *ahh* over. To my own surprise, I had absolutely no doubts about her, the woman with whom I absolutely knew I wanted to share every day of the rest of my life. She had a vibrant faith, a sharp intellect, a playful wit, and she brought boundless joy to even the most mundane corners of my life. No, it was her gender that meant I needed to be sure. I'm an evangelical through and through, and I'd been raised to believe that the only kind of life-long intimate partnership that the Bible condoned was a man and a woman in marriage. This, and only this, could be the bedrock of society and the basis of family life—any other kind of relationship would be a rejection of God's blueprint for humanity.

Many gay Christians, especially those with an evangelical background, have a story of troubled and even tortured teenage years, as they wrestled to come to terms with a truth about themselves that seemed to be utterly condemned by the texts they held so dear. As an apparently straight teenager, I pondered issues of sexuality and Scripture from a safe distance. I searched the Scriptures for principles to follow and found faithfulness, mutuality, and not taking advantage of one another to be the values that should guide my relationships rather than heterosexuality. By the time my attraction to women became clear to me, I had studied at university level the cultural contexts, ambiguous language, and theological threads that had changed my positioning to an affirming one, but other people's opinions took more grappling with.

Church leaders and friends alike expressed their concern that I was straying from God's path. Various New Testament passages were opened for me in hope that I'd heed the warning that homosexual offenders will not inherit the kingdom of God. Because I am bisexual, rather than gay, some implored me to choose to do the "right thing"—to settle down with a man and resist the temptation of women.

So when I'd fallen completely in love and I was ready to propose to this wonderful woman with whom I felt certain God had paired me, I worried that the reaction from Christians with a conservative view would make me doubt myself and doubt my relationship. Would I really always have an answer for those who condemned my love and my life? Before I put a ring on her finger, I needed to hear the go-ahead from God himself. I needed to listen to him with all the humility and obedience of heart I could muster. I needed to give him every opportunity to steer me away from this proposal if that was what he wanted. Only then would I be truly confident, whatever flaming arrows flew my way.

Silence fell. For a week, I tuned out of workplace chatter and the gossip of my friendship group. I switched off from cute family updates and romantic late night calls. I became totally un-contactable to anyone but the Lord. For a week I asked God to speak. I was listening. If there was anything he wanted to convict me of, anything I needed to reconsider, if I'd got it wrong on same-sex relationships—if I'd got it wrong on this relationship—then this was the time for Him to tell me.

And he spoke, through prayer and Bible study and spiritual direction, gently challenging me on unexpected subjects: my fear of making big decisions, for instance. Time and again he gave me the words, "Do not be afraid." With each experience of intimacy with God, each time of worship, I felt only a growing sense of peace and assurance. Still, I wondered if my failure to hear God condemn my relationship was lack of desire to listen. Perhaps I was shutting my ears to his warnings.

On the final night, I took out my Bible once again and opened to Rom 1:18–32. If God wanted to tell me that homosexual relationships were immoral, surely I'd hear him through this passage—others had used it often enough to tell me exactly that.

I traced over the familiar words with my finger. "They exchanged the truth about God for a lie . . . worshiped and served created things rather than the Creator. . . . Because of this, God gave them over to shameful lusts. Even their women exchanged natural sexual relations for unnatural ones . . . men also abandoned natural relations with women and were inflamed with lust for one another."

I listened. Would God condemn me?

In the quiet of my heart, I heard a surprising question: "Do you see yourself here? Does this passage describe you?" I looked again at the descriptions of people who refused to glorify and thank God, who worshiped created things, who had foolish and dark hearts. I considered the years of intimacy and relationship with God I'd had, how worshiping him had sustained me. I considered my painful awareness of my sin, how precious forgiveness and redemption through Christ was to me, and how thankfulness to God was my daily on my lips.

"No." I replied to the Lord. "No, because you are my God. You have brought me to faith, you have taught me to worship—you have poured the light of Christ into the darkness in my heart. To see myself in that passage would be to deny all that you've done in my life. That is not me."

My heartbeat was almost audible. Did I take that conclusion from the text by myself, or did God give it to me? It seemed so obvious when I looked at the words again. There was no way that God counted me as one who didn't know him. No way that passage could be about me. No way that it had been intended to denigrate my love for a woman.

I flipped forward to Gal 5:19–23, another well-worn passage that had been used to frighten me in the past. I read about the contrast between the "obvious acts of the flesh," and the fruit of the Holy Spirit.

Again, the quiet voice came. God whispered, "Where do you see your relationship? Which list describes its fruit?" I compared the two options— impurity, debauchery, hatred, or rage, selfishness, envy, and drunkenness? Those things had certainly featured in my life before this relationship. In seasons of singleness I'd been prone to self-centeredness, and there had been times when my socializing could well have been described as less than pure.

But those things were not the fruit I saw now. Not with her. Rather, the qualities on the other list, the description of the Spirit's fruit, these were what rung true. Love—yes. I saw that in my life now. Joy and peace—absolutely. Being with her brought out the best in me, made me more loving, more patient, more kind, and more faithful than I'd ever been before. I felt more fully alive, more fully myself than I'd known I could be. Wrapped up in her love I got to benefit from the beautiful fruit in her too.

Where my life had been sometimes restless, often lacking in self-control, and filled with more frustration than joy, now I was flourishing. No one who knew the two of us well could deny that God's Spirit was at work in our relationship. The fruit in our lives was tangible.

God seemed to be resting his case. "Don't be afraid," he'd been saying all week. "Don't be afraid of those who use the Bible as a weapon. Don't be afraid; I am for you. Don't be afraid; I am in your love."

Peace filled me and settled with me. That night, I went to sleep content that I would, the next day, ask the woman I loved to spend the rest of her life with me. Now I knew for sure that there would be rejoicing in Heaven.

Claire grew up in the historic city of Bath, England, and spent much of her childhood trying to change the world with her campaigns (mostly unsuccessful) and to tell people about Jesus (again, with mixed results). She continued to aim for both by studying theology at Oxford University and then working in London as an editor for a Christian international development charity. In 2015–16 she was a member of the first cohort of the Archbishop of Canterbury's quasi-monastic community, the Community of St. Anselm. With her partner Rose, Claire moved to England's post-industrial northeast to begin their journey together in full-time ministry in the Church of England—still trying to introduce people to Jesus and change their little bit of the world.

Finding Faith in *oblivion*

Jonathan Brower

I didn't know when I stepped down from ministry and left my church on the way to coming out at twenty-six years old, that I would lose the loving community that had walked with me since I was nine. I despaired as I watched my newfound openness to my sexual orientation "hurting" so many of my close Christian friends on such a personal level. I didn't want to lose them so I started to accept invitations for coffee to save these friendships.

During dozens of these "coffee meetings," I learned that they needed to tell me how wrong I was and that they couldn't condone my behavior and my lifestyle. To them I was compromising my faith. To me, I didn't know what lifestyle they were talking about and their stance against me made it agonizing to stick around. This wasn't unconditional love. They didn't want to listen to anything but proof, and I didn't have it. I couldn't have had it, after having just left a church where the phrase "if you're too open minded your brains will fall out" was commonly uttered from the pulpit. It was a miracle that I fell in love with a man, opened my heart, and stepped over my brain and out into the secular world. I wasn't initially stepping away to leave my faith, I was moving into a world where questioning was valued and not feared. After six months of these coffee meetings, where friends continued to exert their power and rightness over me and dismiss my faith, my heart metaphorically stopped. I had heard so many times that I couldn't possibly have known God and that he was disappointed in me, that I started to believe they were right. Their ears were deaf and their mouths were loud. I tucked the grain of hope I had that maybe God celebrated me as a gay man, and put it beside the fear that had been planted that told me by embracing my homosexuality I was going against God's will.

Those two messages would battle inside me for years to come and many times I didn't know which side I was on. I was wrecked, uncertain, alone, and most of all exhausted. I closed off my heart to preserve what was left of it and walked away from those relationships. They couldn't see that my love for Jesus was just as pure as the day I first believed, and with their influence, neither could I. There was no place in heaven for someone like me. I had already lost so much of myself fighting against my sexual orientation for fifteen years that I didn't have the strength to fight anything anymore. All I wanted then was peace and that meant everything had to go. So, I left my faith because of my inability to reconcile my sexual orientation, and then I wrote a play about it. In the following excerpt from the play, the characters Tim and Simone are standing on an altar. Simone is about to lead Tim in a ceremony to remove his faith.

SIMONE
Do you wish to receive this life anew?

TIM
I do.

(Simone reveals a pill in her hand)

SIMONE
Love lead him to the waters where he is reborn, so he may be received into the family of the world.

TIM
As it was in the beginning.

SIMONE
Memory of faith, we cast you out, in the name of love. Depart and stay far away, for it is love who commands you. We pay homage to the living community (she looks to the audience) who witnesses your way to freedom.

TIM
Their love will be my freedom. Their love will be my salvation.

SIMONE
Who will see you? Who will welcome you—the newborn. Who will write love upon your heart?

(to the audience)

If he stands before you—a blank slate—will your love come without condition?

(A pause, as if the audience has responded)

So be it. This was your faith, which is no longer for you. Take this and do not remember.

(Tim kneels, holds out his hands. Simone gives him the pill)

May it be for you likewise a gift that foreshadows everlasting love. Amen.

TIM
Amen.

SIMONE
Peace be with you.

TIM
And also with you.

(Simone turns back to Tim, kneels and takes his hand)

SIMONE
I shall see you again, my friend. Go in peace and may love be with you.

(Simone exits)

PART 2: RECONCILIATION

TIM
As I was in the beginning . . .

(Tim swallows the pill. Simone and the others stand to watch in anticipation, concern, and grief. Tim lowers his head and closes his eyes and then he is still. After a long pause, Tim opens his eyes and becomes aware of the audience. He smiles, friendly and wide-eyed like a child. With excited innocence and sincerity he speaks directly to them.)

TIM
Hi. My name's Tim.

(Tim looks over the audience to take them in)

It's nice to meet you.

(The other actors move to surround Tim. All turn to face the audience and in unison, with Tim, all say:)

The beginning.

(Blackout)

It is Pride 2015 in Calgary, Alberta, Canada, and I am sitting in a chair on the altar of Hillhurst United Church—the very church that gave me a home when I felt like there was no church community that could love me. There are close to two hundred people in the audience and all eyes are on me. Beside me sits the creative team for *oblivion*, the semi-autobiographical play I've written about my struggle to reconcile my faith and my sexual orientation. This is an experiment in two acts. The play has just ended with the main character choosing to remove his faith. Together with my creative team, we are about to start the second act, the part of the show where the audience shares their reactions. But before we start, I pause to see who is here. I take a breath and gaze out as if looking for my beaming parents after a show-stopping musical number. I can feel the anticipation for what comes next after the cliffhanger I left them with at the end of Act One. I am struck by the diversity of the audience. One quarter of attendees are from the church community but they are scattered amidst others waving pride flags, wearing rainbow sweaters, and sporting unicorn glitter-painted cheeks. I know some of these people from the theater community and the queer community, and then I see some from my old fundamentalist church. Why have they come? Why has anyone come? This is not an easy topic. People are raw at the best of times about this. There are multiple faiths represented, and there are atheists, people of color, seniors, and teenagers. There's a plethora of impressive hair, business suits, and plaid. There are young mothers, gay couples, straight singles, and inevitably somewhere in the mix are a few Calgary Flames fans. Everyone is sitting beside one other inside a mainline Christian church oblivious to the irony that is their current co-existence. It's like being on a bus or in a coffee shop, except more diverse, and I have everyone's rapt attention. They have all come for my story.

I consider pointing out the obvious: that they all clash terribly and that outside this room they are not in the slightest position to be friends, but I reconsider. I am just grateful they are here, because something big has just happened to this room of people and I can see it on their faces: pure empathy. Wet eyes glisten while others continue to host a stream. Several people hold each other and some look tired and shaken. What I can tell you concretely is that collectively, each individual in the room has just become intensely intimate with the characters in the play and therein somehow intimate with each other. At the same time, I have just re-lived some of the most painful moments of my life. How is my story this powerful? Can it be that this is important to these people's journeys? Is it possible that witnessing my own story is healing my wounds?

Instead of asking the well-worn question, "Can we be healed of our homosexuality?" *oblivion* flips this question on its head and asks, "Can we be healed of our faith?" In the play the central character Tim battles with his religious past that continues to cause challenges in his same-sex relationship. The partnership is healthy but the internal monologue of religious shame that plays on repeat is taking a toll. At this point in his life, Tim has been so unsuccessful in his attempts to reconcile his faith and orientation that he feels his only option for peace is to take a pill that will completely eradicate the part of his identity that is causing him so much pain: his faith. Sound familiar? Those of us who have experienced this struggle, or know someone who has, know that there is always residue left behind; there is no complete erasure of what has come before.

PART 2: RECONCILIATION

I wrote the play in the midst of having rubbed shoulders with many who had experienced dramatic loss. At the time I was no longer calling myself a Christian, and I didn't know what I believed anymore. Meeting with others like me, I found that most ex-Christians had either left their faith because of their gender identity or sexual orientation that didn't "fit" with God's "intention" or they had found that the church's stance on the LGBTQ2+ community was so despicable they could no longer bring themselves to believe in that version of God. There was so much hurt that I wondered how we could ever talk about what we had been through and have others truly understand. We needed a voice and the answer was to take my drama and turn it into art.

Theater amplifies the power of story. It has made me powerful. From my lived experience trying to erase my sexual orientation to the painful decision to step away from the faith, these words from my mind move to the page and are then breathed to life by actors. The word is made flesh. This is incarnation. Add to this a live audience and a creative team and immediately there is community. A beautiful mismatched set of beings experiencing one story together and reflecting, even contemplating, what it means to be human. For a tiny moment in the space of our lives, we are introduced as intimate friends to the inner workings of other people's lives. This becomes most powerful when the truth of their reality seeps into our own and we start to understand, to humanize the "other."

In constructing the play, I chose to end at the moment Tim's faith was erased; leaving it up to the audience to imagine what happened next. I did this because I still couldn't imagine a life where I truly had no spiritual reference—where I was a completely blank slate; I didn't feel I knew yet what Act Two could look like. Somehow I could not bring myself to fully let go of my own faith completely in spite of the tremendous discrimination and harm I had been through. Somehow I held out hope for a better second act. Don't we all? This cliffhanger ending would be the magic catalyst for life-giving conversation around the play's themes in the second act, a moment for the audience to hear each other and respond to the call to action. Specifically, "If he stands before you—a blank slate—will your love come without condition?"

What amazed me as we toured *oblivion*, was the affirming "YES!" that audiences from all walks of life were able to answer to the above question. Atheists, who had dismissed faith, were telling me they now saw the importance of it through the show and were humbled by the love they heard from the Christians that attended. Non-affirming Christians were lamenting and asking forgiveness for how hurtful they'd been. Those who had personally experienced a similar story were feeling seen and heard and were processing their grief. Straight parents finally understood something they hadn't been able to get to through mere conversation with their queer children. Relationships were being restored and bridges built between communities that hadn't previously understood each other. Even our actors were feeling like this was a powerful work of art. All the while, I was this post-Christian guy watching all this happen and thinking, this queer play by a queer playwright is bearing good fruit. Is this ministry? I realized that I was unintentionally evangelizing the church through theater and the power of my story. I did not realize that I was also evangelizing myself.

One night, after listening and responding to some challenging and important questions about the show and its "unhappy ending," I was handed a gift from the audience. I really had thought that Tim was leaving his faith to be an atheist and that the show was about giving other people a window into understanding how messy it is to be caught in the culture wars of LGBTQ2+ identity and Christianity. That was still true, but it was no longer a sad ending for me. Instead, what I now saw clear as day was that Tim was doing what he had to do at that moment to survive. He was removing the toxic belief system that held him captive from seeing any other way forward. What was next was truly his choice, and it would be the response of the people around him that foreshadowed what he would do. If they loved unconditionally, he may find his way to a new understanding of faith. If they continued to shout at each other and ignore his experience, he would fare better in the secular world. I had written an ending that was a metaphor for a new beginning. It was no longer about complete loss, but about hitting the reset button.

I now saw the gift it had been that I'd left my faith behind, because that version of God truly needed die to make way for a new understanding. Gracious uncertainty was my time away from Christianity; witnessing was my opportunity to listen to all sides and choose my new perspective. My own play and the response to it, as people met my characters and experienced empathy, had become my olive branch. I had left my faith and wiped the slate clean, and five years after leaving the church I found myself opening up to a new understanding of God. I would have never got there if I hadn't left in the first place.

Many people want the ending of *oblivion* to tie up all the loose ends. I get this. I did too. I want to experience a narrative that doesn't ask me to question myself too much. I am less and less accustomed to welcome the "to be continued" and more prone to Netflix bingeing. However, I have found that the key to empathy and to loving the "other" is to sit in the tension. That's when I really start listening to the story. Bearing witness, I realize my areas of complicity and my responsibility to do better, to love more fully, and to welcome those on all sides as if my love was the first thing they experienced after wiping their own slate clean.

Tim's story isn't over and neither is mine. The unexpected living Christ who showed up in my play is slowly courting me again, nursing me back to health. I guess when I wrote a play asking Jesus where He was in all this, I should have expected He might show up in the audience and make sense of it all.

Jonathan Brower is a Canadian theater artist who uses art as a vehicle for empathy, education, and activism. He holds drama and communications degrees from the University of Calgary and is pursuing a Masters in Social Justice & Equity at Brock University. Jonathan creates and advocates for queer art that showcases a diversity of cultures, stories, and voices. His quarter-century journey to self-acceptance led him to write *oblivion*, a play that illuminates the pain and complexity of trying to reconcile faith and sexuality. *oblivion* tours as a resource for faith communities looking to engage in dialogue about LGBTQ2+ inclusion. Jonathan and his partner Kyall currently live south of Toronto in the heart of Canada's wine region with their mini palm tree named Fern. Find Jonathan at jduncanbrower@gmail.com or @RegardingDis.

Oh Wait, That's Me

Matthias Roberts

There are times I forget I'm gay.

It's not hard to do. I'll be walking the rainy streets of downtown Seattle with my new bag slung over my shoulder and the fashionable raincoat that was oh-so-difficult to find and I'll feel normal. People will smile at me. I'll smile back, or at least, I think I'm smiling. Until my boss tells me later "I saw you walking on 1st today! You look so angry when you walk around." I thought I was being friendly, but then, he probably didn't see me when I waved at that dog.

I've been waiting for a long time to feel normal. In the world from which I came, normal had very strict boundaries. We called it "biblical." Manhood, womanhood, marriage, whatever—in order to be normal it had to fit within a certain framework. I didn't. If you look through my mom's photo albums from my childhood, you'll find me wearing princess dresses and full makeup posing with my sisters. No wonder my aunt wasn't surprised when I sent her that email telling her about my "same-sex attractions." I'm still a little bit annoyed it wasn't a shock. I thought I had been hiding it so well behind that awful orange community theater curtain.

I grew up in the Midwest. More middle than west. Smack dab in the center of a cornfield in Iowa, give or take some years in Wisconsin. My family was deep within the clutches of conservative Christianity. Normal wasn't an option for me. It was only something to observe and attempt to mimic. What do the other boys like? Oh, okay, I like that too now. "Hillary Duff? I adore her!" Wait, not like that. Apparently the guys in my Boy Scout troop didn't dream of being Lizzie McGuire on stage singing "What Dreams Are Made Of" from the classic movie where she visits Rome.

Normal meant squeezing and pushing and diminishing every single part of me that was different until my outside shell fit and my inside didn't exist. I still get told every once in a while, "I'd have no idea you were gay unless I had asked!" That puzzles me. They must at least wonder? I don't think people generally go around inquiring about sexual orientation. But, I'll take it. Because I still get a strange sense of pride from passing as straight, even if only somewhat. You can probably call that internalized homophobia. It's something I'm still trying to get over. And no, it's not a fear sent from God to show me the error of my ways. Want to talk about demons? Let's talk about a culture that teaches people who are different to hate themselves.

In order to fit in, I had to learn the language and talk about girls as if I were really into them. I had to learn how to smile and push away any and all attraction that might appear when a really hot guy in youth group started talking to me. I'd usually just avoid him; he'd probably call me a girl anyway. Being attracted to men was always on my mind. Hyper-vigilance. No one could ever find out. Intense hatred and fear directed at my little body that had no idea what was going on.

I had no idea what was going on.

It amazes me that I can now walk through the Seattle mist and not give my being a second thought. I'll breathe in the salty air from Puget Sound, grab some flowers from the market, and arrange them on the IKEA table in the tiny downtown studio apartment I rent. It's a life I've dreamed of and here it is, happening now.

A few months ago, I went on my first date, ever. He didn't know that. My therapist tells me I have a preoccupied attachment style, which means I have a hard time believing I'm worthy of love. That feels true to me. There are times I wonder why I can't find goodness within myself, especially in regards to someday actually being in a relationship with a man. But, then I remember the first twenty-two years of my life were filled with messages that told me explicitly that I couldn't love. No wonder I have work to do.

That first date was magical. I had to keep reminding myself it was actually happening, it felt so natural and normal. Fluid. Like the water that runs down my umbrella when I decide I just cannot stand being a pretentious Seattleite who "doesn't use an umbrella." We went to the restaurant where I work. I had a gift card leftover from last Christmas. It spent ten months sitting on my desk collecting dust because I kept projecting a hope that I'd get to use it on somebody special. Two hours into the meal, I spotted

Chef spying on us from across the room divider—he didn't think I noticed. "You two were just so lost in each other's eyes."

That makes me roll the blue eyes I'm just learning to see as an attractive feature of my face. When a person spends years hearing he is unworthy of romantic relationship, the self-loathing doesn't just magically disappear. I don't know if I was lost in his eyes. I thought that was something that only happens in the movies. But the idea of seeing myself so wrapped up another's eyes makes my stomach jump with giddiness. His eyes are really beautiful. Is this what high schoolers feel like when they fall in love for the first time?

Love is a strong word. There wasn't a second date. That felt mature and healthy to my adult-brain. But, a part of me still felt stuck in adolescence. Why couldn't we have just called ourselves boyfriends immediately? He didn't want a relationship. When I stopped and wrote a list about what I actually wanted, like my therapist told me to do, I'm not sure I wanted to be in a relationship either. There's a disconnect. I feel like there are some things I should have learned years ago and I have no idea what they are.

Sometimes I'll overhear a conversation in the coffee shop I frequent about LGBT people and how they're trying to ruin the world. It's not a secret this shop had loose ties to a certain church dynasty that came crumbling down a couple years ago. I go anyway. I really like their coffee. I also really like the chicken nuggets at that one place we were supposed to boycott too. Whoops.

My ears will perk up, like they always do when I hear anything resembling a conversation around sexuality. Fascinating, I'll think, these people are just so different than me. Oh wait, I'll pause, that's me. I'm the person they're referring to. The one who's trying to ruin the world one mocha at a time. I forget about that.

There are so many who are back where I used to be, never able to forget, always remembering they're different. It doesn't matter how many welcome mats a church puts out, or how many times "safe" is used in a conversation. If one has to hide who they are in order to fit in, none of those sentiments make any difference. They just rip apart even more. I'm trying to find all the pieces and put myself back together.

I burst into tears the morning after the date. The sobbing surprised me. I had just put on one of my favorite worship albums and as I went into the bathroom to pee the tears started escaping. I barely even had time to grab my already-wet towel from my earlier shower. I moved to my bed, clutched my pillow, and wrenched for a half hour. Deep soul-level tears. An emotional escape I didn't even realize I needed. Yet, that in itself is something I'm learning to celebrate. I spent eleven years of my life unable to cry. When you cut off one part of yourself, you often cut off many others as well.

I don't even know why I was crying. I texted my friend who is also a crier and she just said, "welcome to the club." I think my therapist would call this congruence. I'm not sure if I like it—bursting into tears while peeing is not an experience I want to become commonplace in my life. The tears themselves though—the saltiness, the way they soak into my pillow and make it all wet — they remind me of the salty wetness of this city that is helping me make all things new.

There's a verse I was reading the other day: "be transformed by the renewing of your mind." I never imagined renewal to consist of salt and dampness and pillow clutching. Or staring a boy in the eyes over steak for three hours. And yet, I feel the newness, the freshness. I feel. And I'm not faking it. There is room to be unhappy; there is room to be angry. I don't have to pretend. I can walk down the street without a smile on my face. I can wave at a dog and feel a burst of happiness.

There are times I see myself as if I were watching a movie. There's that boy walking down 1st with his beautiful raincoat and brand new bag. I'm not sure he's the main character, but he's learning to be. It's the kind of movie where boys do get lost in each other's eyes and the characters, all of them, live happily ever after in the glorious messiness of their lives. There's that boy, he's so . . . gay.

Oh wait. That's me.

Matthias Roberts is a writer and speaker advocating for change in how people in faith communities engage with LGBT people. As a graduate student at the Seattle School of Theology and Psychology he is studying the intersections between sexual/gender identity, psychology, and theology. He blogs at www.matthiasroberts.com.

The Amazing Invisible Bisexual Christian

Kathleen Jowitt

When I came out the first time, I was engaged.
No. When I came out the first time it was as simple a thing as a note in my diary, so matter-of-fact and low-key that I missed it when I was writing the first draft of this essay.

When I came out the second time, I was engaged. Sometimes I say, only half-joking, that it was because I was engaged that I came out: the marriage preparation course made me take a long, hard look at myself, and acknowledge some significant parts that I had previously been ignoring. I don't think that was what the Church of England intended. From this distance, I don't care. The only thing that matters now is that I came out to my fiancé. I wanted to be sure, before we took this step, that we both knew who I was.

Perhaps it isn't so unusual. Of all the L, G, B, or T Christians I know, the huge majority are bisexual women. The majority of those are in opposite-sex relationships. One of them got married a couple of years ago. It was a church wedding and the priest wore a rainbow stole. Perhaps it's easier knowing that one does, after all, have the option of passing as straight if it gets as bad as all that. I don't know. In my experience, passing as straight is almost as tiring as repeatedly coming out.

I am a bisexual Anglican. I know bisexual Catholics, Methodists, Quakers. There are lots of us. We are not obvious, but we are there. I thank God—quite literally—that I was not brought up a biblical literalist, not believing that I had to follow every single verse of the Bible to the letter, particularly the ones in Leviticus and Romans. It saved me a huge amount of angst. I was quite happy being Christian and bisexual. I could see no conflict between these two parts of my identity, so long as I was living a life of sexual and emotional integrity. I was—except for the fact that I knew people were assuming I was straight.

The next time I came out I was married and very aware of my privilege. The question of same-sex marriage was dominating the news then and I was passionately—if silently—in favor of it. I had been lucky enough to fall in love with somebody I could legally marry. I knew how easily it could have gone the other way.

My church held an evening debate to discuss what the parish's position should be. I didn't speak. I didn't need to. It was the sort of church where intelligent people put across coherent, convincing arguments for same-sex marriage as a matter of course. I didn't feel that I had anything to add. At the same time, I would have liked to have spoken because I would have liked to be out. I didn't really regret it, though, until I was walking home with a couple of other people who'd been there.

"I don't know," one said. "I'm not sure it's the same thing. Is it really what these people want?"

I should have said—I wanted to say, "But it's not 'these people.' It's me. It could very easily be me." But I couldn't. I was very invisible then.

I went to see the rector soon after that. I did that every couple of years. He was very good at helping me unravel what was going on in my mind. This time, I had one thing on my mind.

"I feel that I ought to come out," I said.

He pounced on that. It turned out that the two most important words in that sentence were not "come out" but "ought to." I felt that I ought to come out because otherwise I was contributing to bisexual invisibility. I'd got so hung up on my identity as a walking, talking political campaign that I'd completely lost sight of what I needed to do as one individual bisexual.

We did a lot of untangling and separated the guilt around being invisible, the fear around being out, and the vital point that I'd somehow managed to miss—that I didn't actually have to be out if I wasn't ready to be out, that other people were going to think things about me that weren't necessarily true and that it wasn't my job to police their thoughts. That I was where I needed to be.

I didn't come out again for quite a while after that, but I stopped feeling so awful about that.

Another couple of years on, I'd moved job and house and region. I was a new face and rather to my surprise, I was invited to join a prayer group. Apart from anything else, I was impressed at their having pegged me as a Christian without any physical giveaway. I hadn't worn a cross or spoken of belonging to any church. Having entered a new phase of my life with joyous expectation and the intention of saying "yes" to everything I could reasonably say "yes" to, I joined. I wanted to give it a try, no matter how much I suspected it wasn't going to be my style.

It wasn't my style. That much became obvious in the space of my first meeting. Still, style isn't everything and this was an enthusiastic and welcoming group. The prayer was heartfelt and the Spirit was among us. There were a few prayers that made me a little uncomfortable, but on the whole I was able to take the Spirit rather than the letter and say "amen" to that. So it went on for perhaps four or five meetings until I hit my personal barrier.

The petitioner asked the group (all women) to pray for "our men." "Our men" were not, she felt, acting as God intended, not fulfilling their ordained role as head of the women. That got my hackles up, but it was only the start of it. She went on, "they're falling in love with each other. . ."

It's not that she trailed off there. I just can't remember anything else of what she said. I can't remember how the leader turned that into a prayer. I can't remember any more words. I only remember the white heat of anger rising within me. I remember pelting away from that room, swirling up the stairs like lava from an erupting volcano.

I am still proud of the email that I wrote to resign from that group:

> Dear friends,
>
> I am emailing to let you know that I will not be attending the prayer group from now on.
>
> I felt that I could not say a sincere "Amen" to some of yesterday's prayers. We spoke of how God cannot be disillusioned in us, because God has no illusions about us. I am bisexual and I cannot pray for this to change, either for myself or for others, because I know God's peace in accepting this identity. God sees to the heart of me and loves the creature that He made.
>
> I will continue to pray for you all, but it is best for all our sakes that I do this alone.
>
> In Christ,
> Kathleen

When I wrote that I considered glossing over my own sexual identity. There was quite enough to justify my never going back, but it was a now-or-never moment. If I didn't tell these people, I might never tell anyone again. I wanted them to know that there were other ways to be, that it was possible to be Christian, bisexual, and comfortable.

I have not gone back. This is not quite the end of the story. A few weeks later, the woman who had first said those things sent me a link to a broadcast by an American evangelical preacher. I did not listen to it. A friend listened to it for me, and confirmed that I had been right to trust my instincts, and avoid having to listen to things like "the opposite of homosexual is not heterosexual, the opposite of homosexual is holy." I emailed back, explaining that it was offensive and hurtful, and asking her not to send me anything like that again. I tried to receive what I had been given in a spirit of gratefulness for her concern and to reject the offensive, hurtful wrapping paper with love and grace. It is about as difficult as it sounds.

Now I've found a church and sometimes I wear a cross that hangs from a rainbow bead. I'm letting people draw their own conclusions.

Where next? I want to be permanently, irrevocably, out at church, to stop having to tell people. I want to continue working within the Church of England to make it more inclusive and welcoming. I would like to find or set up a network of bisexual Christians, a place where we can just be ourselves.

I want to trust that, even on the days when I'm too tired to argue, when I'm too hurt to forgive, when I'm too scared to be out, my being there at all is helping, somehow. Amen to that.

Kathleen Jowitt is an author and trade union officer. Her first novel, *Speak Its Name*, explores the interplay between Christianity and sexual identity in the context of student life and politics. She lives in Cambridge, UK, and identifies as bisexual and Anglican.

On Being a Professional Queer Christian

Rev. Dr. Neil G. Cazares-Thomas

I was raised in England in the Church of Jesus Christ of Latter Day Saints, otherwise known as the Mormon tradition. My mother and father converted to Mormonism before I was born. They had previously been, at least nominally, Anglican (Church of England). I have said many times before, anything was more exciting than the Church of England. The Mormon church presented something that was lacking in their spiritual life.

I am one of seven children, my identical twin brother and I being the youngest. I have five brothers and one sister, so we fit into the Mormon family identity very well. By the time I was two years old, my mother and father had divorced but we remained members of the church.

My early memories of the church are very good. Unlike many of my contemporaries raised in other parts of the world, especially those in evangelical and fundamentalist churches in the United States of America, I survived very well.

By the time I was about nine years old, my mother had met someone she wanted to marry. In planning to do so, she visited with the bishop at our local Mormon church to discuss being married there. The bishop informed her that marriage was only permitted for members of the church. Because my soon-to-be stepfather was not a Mormon, this was not allowed. After many years of faithful church attendance, tithing, and involvement at many levels, she was rejected and told that her marriage was not good enough. These were words I would later hear about me. The treatment of my mother by the church taught me a valuable lesson.

PART 2: RECONCILIATION

We left the Mormon church and, like so many others, became a family that was not affiliated with any church or spiritual community. The church had given up on my mother and we had given up on the church. I learned that the church was an institution made up of human beings with human-made rules and regulations. No matter how hard I tried, I could not find anything in the text I held sacred that justified this treatment of our family by the church.

Fast-forwarding a few years, I was beginning to understand that my sexual orientation was not quite the same as my siblings. I watched my brothers and sister date people of the opposite gender, while I felt attracted to those of the same gender.

I had only heard negative things about homosexuality in England from more evangelical churches. As I had left the Mormon church at an early age, I had not heard anything directly. Therefore, I suffered very little from toxic theology. That all changed when I came out and discovered the world of religiosity.

Fortunately, coming out at fifteen was a good experience, though I will spare you the details. To the vast degree, my family were very supportive. I eventually found myself at my local Metropolitan Community Church in my hometown of Bournemouth, England. It was a small church filled with people committed to the life of Jesus and how to make Jesus real in their life.

My mother has always told me there was something different about me. She was not referring to my sexuality but to my spirituality. Even after leaving the Mormon church, I would long to be in worship. On Sundays, I would take myself off to any local church: Baptist (not to be confused with Southern Baptist), Methodist, Church of England. I would try them all and enjoy the music, fellowship, and preaching. I have always felt a call on my life to the professional ministry. Now a member of MCC, I entered seminary in England at eighteen. I graduated at twenty-two and was ordained at twenty-three. I have served the church for twenty-seven years thus far.

Seminary was where I first encountered toxic theology. I entered seminary as an out gay man and never tried to hide my sexual orientation. Studying among other seminarians from many different denominations demonstrated to me just how toxic theology can be. A place of liberation often becomes the most controlling place on earth. Ironic, really—and hypocritical.

During the day, I would be told I was an abomination. At night, those same men would want to "come and talk to me" about their own homosexual feelings. Sad and frightening.

I have since pastored two churches and recently began pastoring my third. I served the first, in Bournemouth, England, for twelve years. I served the second, Founders Metropolitan Community Church in Los Angeles, California, for nearly fourteen years. They were both great experiences. I had the distinct honor and opportunity to work with many LGBTQ peoples harmed by toxic theology and religion. I have watched lives transform on a journey to wholeness as they come to a progressive understanding of God, Scripture, and themselves.

I have married, buried, and baptized. I have been a part of many conversations with more conservative Christians and leaders who were open to understanding and journeying with me toward making room at the table for more of God's people, including God's LGBTQ people. I have watched the Holy Spirit generate a spirit of radical inclusion. I have had the great privilege of working with that same Holy Spirit in literally saving people's lives who, because of religious baggage and toxic theology, were contemplating suicide. And, I have grieved the loss of many who chose that path when the burden was too great, when they believed the God of love could, somehow, not love them.

This damage and abuse of Christianity by some is the sin of the church. That sin is not only committed against those who are LGBTQ. Besides homophobia, biphobia, and transphobia, it is evident in the sins of racism, sexism, misogyny, and many other labels used by culture and the church to demonize "other." The people Christ came to love are the ones the church is rejecting. "The stone the builders rejected has become the cornerstone" (Ps 118:22). It is because of this that I continue the work that I do.

In 2008, I graduated with my Doctor of Ministry from San Francisco Theology Seminary, a Presbyterian school in Marin County, California. In June 2016, I was elected senior pastor of Cathedral of Hope United Church of Christ, a 4,500-member congregation in Dallas, Texas. It boldly claims as its mission: "Reclaim Christianity as a faith of extravagant grace, radical inclusion, and relentless compassion."

Again and again, I return to the experience of my mother all those years ago. She was told her marriage was not good enough and contrary to God's word. I remind myself there is a big difference between "churchianity" and "Christianity." I hold to my deep faith in Jesus who commands us to "love God, love others, love self." I call myself back to the simple knowledge that God is love and instructs us to "love one another as I have loved you." These simple truths are truth for us all, regardless of age, color, gender, gender-identity, class, physical ability, education, health status, etc. This is the work of the Spirit. This is the work of the followers of Jesus.

Today, I am bold enough, confident enough, and loved enough to know that Christianity is a lifestyle choice you put on every day. I can reject the dogma of religion established to keep control. I can live by the values of Jesus that always lead to freedom, authenticity, light, and love.

Hallelujah!

The Reverend Dr. Neil G. Cazares-Thomas is the senior pastor of Cathedral of Hope of Dallas, called and elected by the 4,500-member congregation on April 12, 2015, following a year-long search. He began his tenure on June 3, 2015. Dr. Cazares-Thomas previously served for thirteen years as the senior pastor of the Founders Metropolitan Community Church, Los Angeles, the founding church of Metropolitan Community Churches, an international movement of churches reaching in and beyond the gay, lesbian, bisexual, trans, queer, questioning, and inter-sex community, and Metropolitan Community Church, Bournemouth, England. A member of Metropolitan Community Churches since 1981, Rev. Neil has served in numerous denominational positions including chair, Board of Ordained Ministries (European District); member, Elder's Task Force on Education; member, European District Committee; member, Board of Samaritan College in Europe; supervising pastor; and ecumenical officer. More recently he has served on the Moderator's Advising Team and consultant to the Office of Formation and Leadership Development. As a native of Bournemouth, England, Dr. Cazares-Thomas was born into the Church of Jesus Christ of Latter Day Saints. His family left the Mormon Church in his early years. He attended St. John's Theological College (Church of England), La Saint Union (Roman Catholic), and King Alfred's College, and graduated with a BA (MDiv [USA equivalent]). In 2002, he enrolled in the doctoral program at San Francisco Theological College (Presbyterian). He graduated with his Doctor of Ministry in October 2009. He has been granted Privilege of Call in the United Church of Christ. Dr. Cazares-Thomas is a contributing author of *Daring to Speak Love's Name* (1993), *From Queer to Eternity* (1997), and *The Queer Bible Commentary* (2006). He has also been featured in a number of journals relating to queer theology and ministry to the LGBTQ community.

All of Me

Kevin Garcia

I had a friend who asked me why I was still a Christian. Despite all that is happening in our culture, despite having to fight at almost every turn to defend my existence as a queer Christian, why? Why do I still decide to work and do life in spaces that don't honor the fullness of who I am? Why not join a tradition that fully honors and includes LGBTQ people of faith?

Trust me, I've asked myself the same question many a time. In fact, I ask it every time I scroll through my Twitter feed and see what some big-name evangelical has said. I ask it when I go to certain church services on Sunday. I ask it when I run into well-meaning pastors who are "loving, but not affirming" of who I am and how I was created to love and connect with others. I must confess, most of the time I don't know. And that lack of answer is accompanied by a groan of self-reproach and my hands thrown in the air in frustration, not in worship.

It would honestly be so much simpler to be a part of a tradition that allowed me to be myself. It would be easier to work without fighting to defend my dignity and my calling, as a baptized person, to be a minister to my community. I wonder what it would be like to not only bring my full self into a space, but to have my full self celebrated by my community.

That's the problem with so many churches these days. They use big buzzwords like authenticity, transparency, or other fluffy notions that circle that same idea of bringing your full self. Granted, it's better than what I grew up with, which was about keeping up appearances, celebrating the blessed life in spite of extreme pain, staying in line, and never asking questions. What so many churches don't realize is they don't believe their rhetoric. When someone like a white, straight, cisgender, male pastor says, "Come as you are," there is a silent question whispered in the hearts of so many hurting and different people, especially LGBT+ folks: "Do you really mean that?"

So many well-meaning Christians will say things like, "You're loved and wanted here." And then when it comes to who and how we love as LGBTQ people, we're blindsided by the ways in which we are restricted. When we refuse to change, our community begins to treat us differently. It's almost as if they want to get us in the door first and then attempt to change us, rather than what Christ does, which is welcome us as we are for who we are.

We have seen what happens with those the church doesn't want or doesn't like. It usually looks painful, ranging from excommunication to being burned at the stake. We know countless stories of those who lost everything because they simply told the truth about who they were.

And so, rather than suffer that pain, we either lie about who we are or we run away from our communities. We hope to forego the pain of rejection by rejecting them first. We separate our lives into quadrants that never touch or intersect. We have our work lives, spiritual lives, church lives, social lives, sex lives, and so on. We separate our good nature from our bad nature. We ascribe everything we don't like about ourselves to our flesh and try to place it on the altar, hoping it simply burns up and goes away.

What we do when we separate our lives in this way is separate our heart. We separate the singular, integrated being that God lovingly crafted. We compartmentalize our pain, opting only for joy, not knowing that they depend on each other. For how can we know the heights of ecstasy if we never know the depths of sorrow? We push away any negative attributes about ourselves, be it jealousy or anger. We say those things aren't a part of us, rather than owning our sins and being able to truly repent.

The same goes with our sexuality. When we divorce ourselves of our natural sexual expression—gay or straight or otherwise—we are deeply affected. By attaching sexuality to our sin nature, our flesh, a thing we want to separate ourselves from, we learn to abhor it. We learn to hate it. We learn that we must kill it.

What is terrifying about this mind-set is the attitude of outright violence toward ourselves. It can manifest itself in addiction to numb our pain or attempt to cope with our personal grief. It can also present in mental illness, actual physical ailments, self-harm, and even suicide.

But we learn to hide behind our desire to belong because that's how we are wired. Especially when you come from a conservative context, you'll do anything to try and play the part.

At least that is what I did.

I made a woman fall in love with me once. I knew all the right things to say, all the right things I should do as a boyfriend and future spouse. I knew about my role as the leader in the relationship. I knew how to honor her and God by abstaining from sex until our marriage night. I knew that this was the path God had for me. I just knew it.

I was in my mid-twenties at the time. After over a decade in ex-gay therapy, I had this frightening realization that my attraction to men would probably never go away. Despite that, I rationalized that just because I happened to be attracted to men didn't mean that I couldn't marry a woman. That was, after all, God's plan.

I had gotten to the point where I could have made that happen. I had done all the right things, taken all the right steps, and meditated on what it was to love someone for all of who they were with all of who you were. That was when I realized I couldn't do any of that, and that everything I did was for the wrong reasons. I was with her because I needed to be assured of God's love for me, not to assure her of my love for her. I was chasing after marriage because that would be the sign of my faithfulness to God, not my undying devotion to her. I could never love her fully because I didn't even like myself a little. I could never love her fully because I simply couldn't. I wasn't created that way. I wasn't struggling with my sexuality. I was gay. And it was beyond obvious that nothing, not even God, was going to change that.

Our break-up sent me into a tailspin. I started smoking again. I began drinking heavily. Then, I moved toward entertaining the idea of driving my car into a lake and slowly slipping into nothingness as breath left my lungs. I was beyond disgusted with myself and distraught that I couldn't please God because I couldn't get my flesh under my dominion.

"God, what do you want me to do?" I kept praying that over and over again. And I heard nothing. But I waited because I didn't want it to be a feeling I had or a convincing speech or an argument from a person. I wanted it to be a move of the Holy Spirit that showed me the path forward.

Interestingly enough, I had read a ton of progressive and affirming theology. I understood the arguments for LGBTQ inclusion in the church. I even believed for a while that perhaps God gives some people the freedom to do things, but not others; as if God saved the real suffering for the strongest servants, as if God played favorites, or perhaps that if I suffered the most, I would be more blessed. I wanted it all to be true that I could be gay and Christian, but it couldn't be true for me. I was too unlovely, had done too much wrong, told too many lies, and hurt too many people for my life to ever be redeemed. I saw myself as fundamentally unworthy and broken.

I was so separate from my true nature, from my heart, that I was unable to recognize a self-evident truth that God was trying to speak to me.

The thing about separating our hearts is, in the separation, darkness tends to creep in. The worst words and most horrible feelings and fears take root in the spaces between. These roots trap our hearts, causing them to turn hard toward ourselves. We are unable to see things for what they are, and unable to receive anything new from God.

But there was a truth calling out to me, and I heard its cry, but I couldn't move. I was too paralyzed, too separated from my own heart to understand that voice calling to me was the Spirit deep within, yearning for me to be whole.

But it is in that moment, when all hope is lost and the world is frozen in fear, that God comes in with a river of grace to wash away everything we thought we knew and replace it with a peace to be okay with never fully comprehending.

Shortly after our break-up, I attended a conference. Not knowing what to expect, but desperately needing some answers, I walked into a room full of strangers. I sat a few rows back and just prayed that God would speak. I wanted either the confirmation that I needed to commit to celibacy or that maybe . . .

Maybe something else was possible. Maybe there was a different way to live because, at that point, I didn't know how I could remain where I was.

When the worship music started, I lifted my hands, like I always do, and I just waited. Something happened next that I can't quite describe. My body felt heavy, gently giving way to this waterfall of light and electricity and gold just bearing down on me. It felt warm and bright and full. It engulfed me, and I began to cry silent tears, in awe of the presence that had come to me. It was like nothing I ever felt before.

In an instant, I was filled with a zeal to live like never before, where before I had been so desperate to die. I was confident in the direction my life was headed because I knew it was going to be toward God.

And yes, I get that it sounds like fantasy or perhaps a bit crazy. But, it's no crazier than when my body was healed instantly because we prayed for it. It's no crazier than the spot-on, prophetic words I have received over the years. And it's certainly no crazier than the confession that I believe a rabbi over 2000 years ago, who was executed by the state, rose from the dead and was the literal son of God.

In that moment, there was this sense of wholeness I'd never felt before, a peace that told me this is what I was created for. I came into a space with my full self and allowed myself to be celebrated in the fullness of who I was. I allowed all the aspects of my life that I had separated out to become one again, reuniting me with my Divine design and reconnecting me with my Divine Union with the Spirit.

Since then, I have never been surer of my calling as a son of God. I've never been more compelled by the teachings of Jesus to do good in the world, to strive to walk humbly, live mercifully, or love even those who hurt me. I have never been more connected to the Holy Spirit and the supernatural work done around me, in me, and for me. I feel a fullness and overflowing of God in ways that wouldn't have been possible before when I was living in shame for simply being who I was created to be.

So, why am I still a Christian? Even with all that is happening in our culture, why do I still wear that title? Why do I still decide to work and do life in spaces that don't honor the fullness of who I am?

I'm still a Christian because I've seen too much. I've experienced too much of the fullness of God just to chalk it up to mere coincidence or emotional overstimulation. I've had these weird, mystical, and mysterious things happen to me that are beyond explanation. Sometimes we call things beyond explanation miracles.

I stay in Evangelical circles because it is the Evangelical Church that introduced me to a Jesus who loved the outsider and championed those who were hurting. For better or for worse, they are my family. And I want my family to experience the fully integrated life, the abundant life Jesus talked about.

I'm still a Christian because the church, at its best, can be a force for good in the world. I'm still a Christian because the life, the teaching, the person of Jesus is more compelling than anything I've encountered in this world. And no matter how much his followers screw it up, Jesus holds the promise of redemption.

I do life in spaces that don't honor the fullness of who I am because I don't need another person to tell me I am worthy or welcome. I understand that Jesus welcomes me. The body is for me. The blood is for me. No one gets to tell me that this is untrue. I stay because I see the humanity in those who can't or won't see it in me, and I am called to restore sight to the blind.

All of me is welcome in God's presence, even the parts I don't like; even the parts I wish didn't exist; even my anger, jealousy, and fear. It all belongs and is all needed to be human entirely. My wholeness is my gift to the world. I come as I am, fully and totally myself, as a prophetic gesture of where we are headed as a people. There will be a day when churches everywhere say, "Come as you are," and mean it completely, for everyone, without exception.

It is a day that I long for and I believe is not so far away. And with every breath I have on this earth, I will tell my story so that others might be able to experience the same joy and freedom of coming as their full self into the presence of God, into abundant life.

That is why I am still a Christian.

Kevin Garcia is a writer, blogger, podcaster, and creative who is making his way into full-time content creation, making videos, blogs, and podcasts that reflect the diverse LGBTQ+ experience. Since graduating from Christopher Newport University in 2013 with a Bachelor of Music, he's been everything from a voice coach, to a missionary, to a corporate office worker, to a barista, and everything in between. Since coming out as a gay Christian in fall 2015, he's connected with thousands of people through his blog and podcast, hoping to empower people to live a fearlessly authentic life while helping to create safer spaces in Christian communities. He blogs regularly at theKevinGarcia.com, hosts a podcast called *A Tiny Revolution*, and leads worship with his small group. When he's not trying to dismantle the white cis heterosexist capitalist patriarchy, you can find him drinking way too much coffee, making tacos, or getting into some form of tomfoolery with his incredible community in Atlanta, Georgia.

Forgiving the Church When It Fails Us

Rev. Erica Lea-Simka

October 2012.

O   "All are welcome here," the church website said.

"Christ's body broken for you," the pastor said as he handed me a morsel from the loaf.

"Was all this true? There would be serious consequences if I came out, and I doubt the pastor was supportive of LGTBQ people because the church is so painfully silent about anything sexuality related or gender related beyond support for women's ordination. Wait . . . did that mean they would support my ordination as long as I went along with the assumptions that I was straight? Could I go along with that anymore? Is it even acceptable for me to accept Communion? Did God accept me? I doubt the church would accept me. . ." I mentally rambled on while "paying attention" during the service.

May 2015.

"All are welcome here," the church website said.

"Christ's body broken for you," I said as I handed each person a morsel from the loaf just moments before I had been officially ordained. Officiating Communion was my first act as Rev. Erica Lea. I had served Communion many times and I had even officiated Communion many times before becoming Rev. Erica Lea. Every time felt sincere and as engaged as possible, but there was something particular about my calling and life's work being affirmed that propelled me forward with new energy.

When I was ordained, the texts included:

> Psalm 27: The Lord is my light and my salvation; whom shall I fear? The Lord is the stronghold of my life; of whom shall I be

afraid? . . . One thing I asked of the Lord, that will I seek after: to live in the house of the Lord all the days of my life.

Acts 2:1–8: The witness of Holy Spirit at Pentecost included echoes of the prophet Joel, "In the last days it will be, God declares, that I will pour out my Spirit upon all flesh, and your sons and your daughters shall prophesy."

John 20:11–18: The witness of Mary Magdalene at the empty tomb. She believed when others didn't. Jesus called her by name for a particular purpose and women like myself have been running to speak truth to power since.

Fearlessness. Empowerment. Protection. Faith. These are my ministry life goals.

I took ordination vows, committing to trust that God has called and gifted me for ministry, to be faithful to the work God has given me, to lead with a Christ-like spirit, to help the church be a community of welcome, justice, grace, love, and peace, and to forgive the church when it fails me.

When the church fails me, not *if*.

A major way the church failed me is by being silently hostile and explicitly hostile toward gender and sexual minorities before I even came out to myself, and even more so after I came out publicly. The church failed me when I desired ordination after serving in different ministries for years, but the structural price to pay of a Texas Baptist church ordaining me if I was out was a higher price than politely sympathetic moderates were willing to pay. Instead, they choose to wait until inclusive ways of doing church and ordination hit the bargain bin so that the price they pay for doing what is right feels more within their comfortable budget.

If Jesus' most important work was relating to people and their maladies, then my most important work as a pastor should be likewise. Jesus lived and taught with mystery, but he did not hide himself. If Jesus lived openly about his radical teachings, then I should follow suit as a teacher of his radical teachings. Seeking ordination while closeted was not an option on the table.

So, I waited. I waited for a church that would ordain me. I waited for a little wiggle room to resist the rigged system set more on self protection rather than Gospel liberation. I waited. I wait.

I hoped my full coming out, serving a welcoming and affirming church, and my ordination would heal the pains of the ways the church failed me. These profound experiences have contributed to healing, yet more healing remains to be seen.

Erica, will you forgive the church when it fails you?

I will, because unforgiveness in my heart damages me more than anyone else.

I will, because the longer I don't forgive, the deeper the spiritual abuse penetrates my mind and spirit.

I will, because to forgive is divine and it is the Divine one who calls me to say, "Christ's body broken for you." And you. And you. And you.

Rev. Erica Lea-Simka is originally from Houston, Texas. She has served Baptist and Mennonite congregations in Wyoming, Texas, North Carolina, and Washington DC, and currently serves as pastor of Albuquerque Mennonite Church. Erica is a graduate of San Jacinto College, Texas A&M University, and Truett Theological Seminary. Her favorite teachers include Flannery O'Connor, Mary Magdalene, and Mollie Katzen. She enjoys cooking, movies, traveling, and time with her sweetheart. Connect with Erica on Twitter (@RevEricaLea) or on her website (revericalea.org).

Good Enough

Darren Calhoun

My personal faith journey began at age eleven when I began to attend church regularly with my mom. We visited a few Catholic churches, finally settling on a church that was just a short drive away from my neighborhood. It was a predominantly black church full of working-class families who saw themselves as good people. There weren't any harsh messages about avoiding anything, and we certainly didn't talk about sex or sexuality. I was very active in leading our youth from the age of about twelve through my freshman year of college.

Toward the end of my freshman year, I came out as gay but I wasn't worried about rejection from people in my church or family. I didn't grow up doing things that might be called typical for a young boy. I was creative and into stage performance. When bullied for not playing sports or just not fitting in, I would cry but my parents never made me feel bad for showing emotion. So, moving into my young adult years, I never doubted that I would be loved by the people who mattered most to me. I generally felt safe at home and church.

I was one of the first people at this small Catholic university to be openly gay (and the only gay person that I knew of on campus). I came out via a poem that included the line "I'm black, Christian, and gay" and shared it at several gatherings and with friends. At the time, I was comfortable with who I understood myself to be and who I was becoming. That all changed during my second year of college.

"What does God want for your sexuality?"

A young man who would eventually become a close friend and with whom I would build a campus ministry asked me that question. It was one

I'd never considered before, and it led to us regularly meeting together for Bible study to explore the answer to that and other questions, along with a growing number of students.

One night, we had an experience that reminded us of the outpouring of the Holy Spirit in the second chapter of Acts. During a Bible study someone in the room began speaking in tongues for the first time, and the minister who was leading the study began to pray over us. Many of us were moved to tears as the minister prayed for specific things that we hadn't shared with her but were exactly the situations happening in our lives. The presence of the Holy Spirit was palpable to us. I walked away from that experience wanting my primary identity to be Christian. I immediately stopped identifying as gay and felt that I'd been delivered from my same-sex attraction. Myself and several of the other students who were part of this Bible study began attending, and eventually joined, the church of my friend who asked me that critical question,"What does God want for your sexuality?"

Like my Catholic church, this new church was also a mostly black congregation, but it was my first experience in a Charismatic/Pentecostal black church. People spoke in tongues and prophesied, the music was loud and often broke out in spontaneous choruses. Crying, dancing, and receiving prayer for healing or deliverance were part of every service. For me, this was very different from my Catholic church upbringing but I enjoyed it and felt energized about getting more involved there.

However, this is also where I first regularly heard harsh messages about "fags in the church" and how homosexuality was a "spirit from the Devil." It was also in this church that the pastor, upon hearing that I had previously identified as gay, pulled me aside and told me that I should "never talk about that again" and that I should be ashamed that I was ever homosexual. He said I should forget it ever happened, because people wouldn't be able to see me as a man of God if they knew that about me.

My pastor delivered this message to me about one month before I was to be ordained as a minister. I was nineteen years old, and suddenly I needed to erase a major theme of my teenage years. This seemed contrary to what I thought was good news, but I was willing to follow this leader because of all the good things that were happening at this new church. I stopped telling my story. In many ways I lost my witness. Without this important part, Darren was just a nice guy who always loved Jesus.

PART 2: RECONCILIATION

Am I Good Enough?

It was Sunday, late afternoon, in the fall. An hour or so earlier I'd served with the ministry team at church, tearfully praying with people from our congregation at the end of the service. This is what I generally did on any given Sunday, including teaching Sunday School and singing with our praise team at our Charismatic, nondenominational church on the south-side of Chicago.

As I was cleaning up the auditorium, the elder who was assigned to work with me in dealing with my struggle with homosexualty came over and said she needed to speak with me. I figured she wanted to follow up with me after my confession to her, a few days earlier, that I'd recently given into sexual temptation. Many words were exchanged during that meeting at the back of our church auditorium, but one thing she said to me still echoes in my head to this day:

"You just don't know how damned you are. . ."

That short sentence, those few words—it was like being hit by a truck. I didn't see this response coming and my mind was reeling with the implications of such a statement.

I knew enough about the Bible to know, on some level, that this wasn't biblically accurate. I wasn't actually damned. Was I? No, Jesus' grace was sufficient for all. But I was also deep-down-to-my-bones convinced that something was terribly wrong with me and I was desperate to find some way to be fit for heaven. After all this time, why couldn't I get rid of this attraction to men?

I'd spent the previous two years living in the basement of the church under constant supervision and before that, four years struggling on my own with prayers and fasting. All of this was an effort to try to help me get "delivered" from the demon of homosexuality or "healed" from the brokenness that caused me to be attracted to the same sex. These two perspectives—healing and deliverance—were commonly echoed but very uninformed answers to homosexuality within the church. Preachers would condemn homosexuality from pulpits and if they offered any solutions, deliverance and healing were the only acceptable options—everything else was seen as compromise and unbelief. If one were to press deeper into the question of what the process for deliverance or healing looks like, the answer would often rest on faithfully pleading with God until something happens. This "solution" was usually offered by people who never faced this issue and some would vaguely reference hearing about someone who had "come out of homosexuality."

Because of the teaching of my church, I was led to believe that to go to heaven, I would have to be heterosexual. Further, our church focused heavily on denying oneself to follow Jesus and I was fully willing to do whatever it took to be faithful. The elder who'd just told me that I was damned would now ask me to leave everything—attending university, my photography business, my friends, and even my family. She said, "If you really want to be saved, then you'll accept this help," and with that plans were made for me to move into a church we had in Indiana where I would be relieved of my ministry duties and live under twenty-four-hour supervision.

I felt like I was somehow letting everyone down because I couldn't fix my attractions. Even though this struggle remained private between the church leaders and me, I felt like I was supposed to be a shining example of righteousness and instead I was a failure.

During these years I took on something I never had before: shame. And shame changed me. Shame made me hide, keep secrets. The shame fueled compulsive sexual behaviors. Shame was keeping me from being known and loved as I am. Church had convinced me that I was unlovable. My daily effort was to not be gay so that I could be loved by God and the more I focused on what not to do, the more likely I was to act compulsively.

In the years I spent pursuing change, I eventually came to realize that God was pursuing me. Because of the culture of my church, I believed God would be distant from me. Instead, God would show up everywhere. When I acted out in sexual compulsion, God would put someone or something in my path to remind me that I'm beloved. When my church leaders condemned me, God would show me that I still have purpose by using me to help someone who was hurting in ways similar to me. God was counteracting all the negative messages I was hearing and believing about myself.

Small promptings from the Holy Spirit sustained me during hopeless nights. When I despaired my life, the Scripture would resonate in my ears:

> For the Lord your God is living among you.
> He is a mighty savior.
> He will take delight in you with gladness.
> With his love, he will calm all your fears.
> He will rejoice over you with joyful songs.

—Zeph 3:17 (NLT)

It became evident to me that God was refusing to give up on our relationship. Day by day I became confident that God is for me and not against me. With time and support from friends, I began to see that the plans to help me at this church weren't going to help at all. In 2005 I moved back to Chicago and found myself unable to tolerate the condemning atmosphere at the church I was once so happy to be part of. When I moved, the church leaders who'd been working with me cut off all direct communication. I'd given up everything for that church and now I found myself without the desire to even attend. I felt more hopeless than ever and seriously wondered if God really wanted me to leave that place.

The Biggest "No" in the Bible

In 2007, I saw a billboard advertising a new church in Downtown Chicago. I began attending this large nondenominational evangelical church. I didn't want to be part of a church where I couldn't be honest about my journey and hoped that authenticity would fare well for me here. When I shared my struggle with same-sex attraction and sexual compulsion with the leaders of that church I was asked to meet with an elder to determine if I would be eligible to serve as a volunteer leader. On the Sunday that the meeting was scheduled, the sermon felt like it was just for me. This sermon was from a series of messages about keywords in the Bible. That day's message was about the biggest "no" in the Bible. I sat near the front of the church crying endlessly through the worship music that opened our gathering. I wondered if I would be condemned again. I wondered if God would use me at this new church that I'd come to love in countless ways. The message turned out to be about Rom 8:1: "Therefore, there is now no condemnation for those who are in Christ Jesus." I was so inspired by such a grace-centered message, but could it really be applied to me—a guy who might be gay?

That afternoon, I sat down with the elder and shared my whole life story. I hoped that if I told him everything there wouldn't be a delay in him rejecting me. The elder listened intently as I shared almost nonstop for two hours. In the end he looked into my eyes and told me, "We all have struggles. We would love to walk along side you in your journey and we'd love for you to volunteer with our arts ministries." He went further to share how he could see that worship was life-giving for me and that the best thing for me would be to offer my gifts in worship. That day I not only felt heard, but also understood. I felt like my struggles weren't in vain. Through the next several years I was renewed in God's love for me and my calling to serve God's people. Through much wrestling through theology, I've come to understand that my sexual orientation can't change God's love for me. I'm now confident that the theology that informed my previous church was toxic and doesn't bear the fruit of the Spirit. Because of love, I'm no longer living in the drive of sexual compulsion. Condemnation and control could never produce the kind of abundant life that God's love and truth bring forth in me now. I'm thankful that my story didn't end with a hopeless struggle to not be gay. Today, I'm both Christian and gay, and I'm free to live a life of love in response to the unending love that God has shown me.

Darren Calhoun is an advocate, worship leader, and photographer based out of Chicago. He works to bridge relationships between people of differing perspectives through story and relationship. Intersectionality is his primary lens when facilitating dialogue and education about justice and inclusion for people marginalized based on race, gender, and/or sexuality. Currently, Darren is Worship Leader at Urban Village Church—South Loop, Associate Fellow at Evangelicals for Social Action, in addition to owning Darren Calhoun Photography and serving on the boards of LGBTQ Christian organizations. He's also an extrovert who loves hugs. Follow him on social media at @HeyDarren or visit his site, DarrenCalhoun.com

Set Apart

Amy Jo Becker

Four years ago, I admitted to myself that I was attracted to women. At the time, I was a worship leader at a Southern Baptist Church, a wife of eleven years, and a mom of two girls, ages three and one. The shame and fear were so great that I checked myself into therapy. I felt my life was ruined. If this thing were true—if, in fact, I was gay—I stood to lose everything. Literally.

You see, I was raised in a fundamental Christian home that was fueled by Calvinism. My loving and well-intentioned parents raised me the way they believed was best, but I only attended private Christian schools, and was only taught philosophies that fit the paradigm of rigid, black-and-white, rule-based salvation. For example, I was not allowed to have a radio until I was fourteen, and even then, I was only allowed to listen to Christian stations. I read *White Fang* in high school, with the curse words blacked out in Sharpie. I was taught very little about evolution, and only with the express purpose of being able to shoot it down in a debate. I did the wholesome Christian girl thing, sincerely and well. I was a "wise" unofficial peer counselor, memorized whole books of the Bible, went to youth group and the girls' Bible study, took notes on sermons, and watched only the movies that James Dobson told my parents were safe for their children. Focus on the Family dictated our family life. My parents gave me a purity ring, I wanted to be just like Elisabeth Elliot, and I "kissed dating goodbye." I wanted to become the wife of a pastor. I was the girl that everyone *wished* their little boy would grow up and marry. I thought I was holy because I didn't struggle with lust for men, like my female classmates. I was curious about sex, of course, but no way I would ask my parents! I couldn't be real with my family; we were plastic: afraid to admit to ourselves or anyone else that we were anything but godly, pure, and happy (because of Jesus' blood sacrifice, of course). Due to this stifling upbringing at home, school, and church, I was *very* unprepared for life in general, naive, and without common cultural experiences with which to relate to anyone outside of the conservative Christian bubble. To this day, I feel I am at a disadvantage in social circles. I graduated from high school without even knowing what homosexuality was . . . except that it was an "abomination" to the Lord.

For three semesters, I attended John MacArthur's The Master's College in California. I didn't know it then, but I was being further indoctrinated into a uniformity that devalued women and filled me with fear-based, graceless religious rules. Then I transferred to Colorado Christian University, which, compared to TMC, was very liberal at the time. I still didn't know anything about sexuality and would sneak to the basement of the library and look up things like "onanism" (masturbation) and "lesbian." I was terrified that someone would find out I was interested in such "ungodly" things, and I never imagined I could possibly be the "abomination" myself. In retrospect, there were signs I couldn't have recognized then, and if I'd had the ability to identify my attraction to women at the time, I would have sought reparative therapy so I could be pleasing to God.

In my senior year, I was exposed to philosophy and twentieth century literature for the first time. I had never heard of such things as fatalistic determinism and nihilism. I was shocked at how well those ideas meshed with my current theology: God "wins" in the end, and only those who were "predestined" would be saved. *So . . . what were we supposed to do with our lives until then?* I felt lost, without meaning or purpose. I lost everything except three core things: 1) God loves all people, me included; 2) we are to love God and love people; and 3) worship, whatever form that takes, is never a waste of time. So why was I pursuing a degree—a piece of paper that proved that I had a certain amount of "human" knowledge? For the applause of fellow humans? So I could score a high-paying job and buy a big house and fill it with meaningless junk? The world seemed to be a superficial superstructure that mankind had invented to give themselves meaning. I barely graduated. I was completely isolated in my plight, afraid to admit aloud that I wondered if everything I had ever been taught was a lie. My advisor connected me with a Christian therapist—a fact I hid from my parents, because "Christians can't trust psychology." As it turned out, not even my Christian therapist was safe for me. I scared the crap out of her, which landed me in a psych ward—another thing I needed to hide from my parents, but failed. I felt like everyone thought I was crazy and deserved to be there. In retrospect, every time I risked telling someone things were unraveling, I was challenging the worldviews of my fellow Christians, which made them uncomfortable.

Shortly after graduation, I met my husband. Falling in love healed a lot of things . . . for a while. I slowly reincorporated my old thinking; I had been well-trained. As a wife, I never enjoyed sex. Hated it, even. I prayed that God would make me like it. I read all kinds of things, mostly Christian, of course, that might help me to be "what my husband needed." I felt like a failure. I thought there was something wrong with me. I thought he was obsessed with sex and had an "unholy" obsession. For thirteen years I tried. And prayed. And tried again. And prayed some more. I was miserable, dreading the next time I would have to psych myself up to be "stabbed" for his pleasure, which was my "wifely duty." We tried everything to make it better. I didn't realize my poor husband felt rejected and shamed by me. We were both in pain, trapped in a seemingly never-ending situation.

My fascination with women never waned. In fact, it intensified. I wondered what it would be like to touch one—kiss one. I secretly watched movies with LGBTQ characters. In 2013, I finally realized I needed some help reconciling this "shameful thing," and checked myself into therapy. When at last I confessed my attraction to women to my husband, he really wasn't surprised. In fact, he'd suspected as much for a while. He was relieved that our "problems" weren't due to any failing on his part, and he felt badly for me—that I was thirty-seven years old and only then figuring out these things about myself.

Understated, the next few years were pure torment, and they almost killed me numerous times. If I was gay, I stood to lose everything that was precious to me: my marriage, our white picket-fence dream, most of my dearest friends, my church, my family, and any ability to please God ever again. *How is this my life? Surely I am not "the bad thing." Who IS this person masquerading as me?* I didn't recognize myself, even in the mirror. The process of accepting my orientation has been excruciating. I had to explore and eliminate every possible cause; I wanted so badly for it not to be true. Eventually I came to realize that I was indeed made this way, and that, as God's handiwork, I am already inherently pleasing. That had to be enough; I could never change either truth, no matter what.

First I came out to my husband's parents. They were shocked and saddened by the imminent changes, but embraced me wholeheartedly. I will be forever grateful to them for the amazing love, acceptance, and support they have extended to us. My parents have been a different story. The chasm that was our already strained and superficial relationship has only deepened. They don't even have to tell me they think I have lost my mind, backslidden, and fallen away from God. I believe they feel they are walking on eggshells, afraid of saying or doing something that might drive me away permanently. This breaks my heart, but I will never doubt their love, conditional as it may be presently. They are trying, but I hate that they have to "try." I hope for the day that they will realize that I did not "choose" my sexual orientation. (And who would? Why would willingly put themselves through the mental, spiritual, and physical anxiety I have endured as I lost almost everything I loved? Who would choose to put themselves into a minority that faces so much discrimination and judgement from the mainstream evangelical Christian world they love?) I long for the day they will realize that yes, my faith looks different now, but it is much stronger than they currently think possible.

Accepting that God is unconditional love, and that "nothing can separate me" from that love, has been the largest leap of faith I have ever made. As I begged God for answers, I realized that if I really believed that the Holy Spirit would not lead me astray, then I should not be afraid to question everything I had ever been taught. The Holy Spirit would guide me. I have discovered that God is *not* retributive, punishing, or blood-thirsty. Realizing the sheer height and depth and breadth of God's love has kept me alive. I cannot help but believe that, had I been better educated as a young woman about sexuality and the role it plays in healthy human relationships, I would have recognized that humans were created to be sexual, and that I was gay, many years ago. Had I not been brainwashed to believe God was all about the arbitrary rules humans have made to control and subject other humans—that God was anything other than pure love for all of creation—my family and I would have been spared some of the torture we have all endured.

Last year, my "wasband" and I held a small un-wedding ceremony for close friends and family. We celebrated what our lives had been up to that point, mourned the death of the dreams we had held for ourselves as a family, and marked the day as a point in time where we publicly chose hope for the future, and declared our commitment to remain close, even as we redefine what "family" looks like for us and our girls. For my thirty-ninth birthday, I gave myself the gifts of authenticity and vulnerability by coming out on Facebook. It was a good decision, one that I do not regret. It helped to heal the internal split that religion had caused within me. It naturally culled the friendships that would cause us further harm, and it allowed me the joyful surprise of dear friends who are determined to stay the course with us in the future. My support system has been refined and my precious new "tribe" keeps growing. I am free.

Let me be clear: this freedom is not without pain and grief. I often mourn the losses I have incurred. Losing friends and family feels terrible. Having your faith judged and losing your "godly" reputation hurts. Starting over is hard. Divorce is heartbreaking; I miss my wasband. He remains my best friend and co-parent, but everything is different. Despite all these things, my freedom keeps growing.

I look forward to the day when "coming out" will not even be a thing. I can't wait until the church can embrace all of creation with the kind of love God does. May my story, my witness, encourage those who are affected by toxic theology. May my experiences help spare other LGBTQ from the shame and self-loathing caused by condemnation from people who believe they have God figured out. May those who are and who love LGBTQ family members be challenged to see the undeniable, unconditional love of God.

Amy Jo Becker is an almost-forty year old, unfundamentalist mother of two magical, sunshine-filled girls, ages seven and four. She has a BA in English Composition from Colorado Christian University. She is an abstract watercolor and acrylic artist, blogger, poet, musician, and photographer, who consistently uses the word "eclectic" to describe all of her styles: profession, parenting, home decor, appearance, literature, music, and faith. She is not a fan of boxes—for God or people. She believes in love, vulnerability, advocacy, equality, coffee with creamer, and candy . . . lots of candy.

Let Not Your Heart Be Troubled

Candace Thompson

What God anoints and appoints cannot be wished or wiped away. As long as I can remember, the Spirit of God has been an active presence in my life. As an infant, I was christened in the Catholic faith. At the age of eight, I was baptized by submersion in the Missionary Baptist faith because the Catholic sprinkles did not stick after my mother remarried. I spent lots of time with my grandparents who were of the African Methodist Episcopal (AME) faith tradition. There was not room "for someone like me" who is attracted to the same gender in all of these faith traditions. These were my formative years.

In my teenage years, I was every youth director's dream. I was active in several ministries and part of a multitude of church happenings. Sunday School, youth choir, church plays, and back-to-back terms as the president of the Youth Department marked my youth. Winning Bible sword drills was my weapon of mass destruction! Some might label me as an over-achiever. Eventually I would realize I was trying to prove my sainthood to my fellow church folks. I thought it was through my actions God would see me and find me worthy of love. I had major issues seeking the approval of others until my mid twenties. I feared disappointing my family, community, and my race. Nevertheless, I was not going to get their approval with this "thing" that set me apart. At the age of ten, I thought death was the best solution. Surely, God would have mercy on me and understand. I had no concept of suicide, but thought if I ceased to live this "thing" would be dead. I did all that I knew to be perceived as "normal." If I pushed it down far enough, I could survive life on the surface. Never mind that my only interest in boys was to beat them in P.E. Never mind how I crushed on the good sisters in the Missionary Baptist church, appreciating the best combination of beauty, brains, and love of God. Ministers thought they were grooming me to be a first lady, but I wanted to be a minister.

The evolution of reconciling my sexuality and faith has been a journey. I have had to face all that I feared from family and community—who say they love me unconditionally. It was their judgment and condemnation that I feared the most. I equated their feelings toward me to be equal to the judgment of God. At fifteen, I had the courage to confide in my best friends about my feelings and all the stress it was causing me. I felt safe and we had kept one another's secrets. I had not given thought to any consequences. However, there were consequences. All communications ceased the next day. No phone calls. No eye contact in the hallways at school. No shared carpool. No sharing the same pew at church. Within a week, my whole world collapsed. My friends were no longer my friends. What was shared in confidence, ended up as church gossip. The adults who poured the word of God into my soul ostracized me. The high hopes and confidence gave way to erosion and disappointment. Who was I separate from my church, family, and so-called friends? My mother comforted me out of pity and shame, hoping it was all a phase. In truth, she feared for her own reputation as if my being a lesbian is a negative reflection of her child-rearing. Neither my father nor stepfather were of any consolation. Both of them had checked out. My grandparents only knew to love me. When things would become emotionally overwhelming, I would often reflect back on the scripture taught by my Granny from the gospel of John 14:1–4.

My relationship status with God was a strong "it's complicated" for the next ten years. A series of events led me back to my first love. I had not strayed too far away, but I knew I had to put great distance between me and the church and the people who caused me deep emotional harm. The damage is done. I carried the scars of rejection and quickly learned that "come as you are" is reserved for the others. I had to check my sexual identify at the door in order to feel welcome in God's house.

In July 2004 I stepped out on faith and embarked on my greatest spiritual revolution. I uprooted and moved to Jacksonville, Florida, to be a member of Catholic Volunteers in Florida (CVIF), a faith-based Ameri-Corps program. I was in a new place and did not know a single soul. The ocean breezes were disarming. I took off my mask to face the realities of my distant relationship with God and sought to live, authentically. I went to Florida to spend a year in service and to escape a life of suffocation by faking it. The time away restored my sense of self and released the judgment and condemnation I adopted to be true. Doing justice, active spirituality, creating community, living simply, and personal growth were the pillars of the program that transformed my life. The year of service affirmed my faith journey and revealed a God more concerned with how I love and live rather than with whom I love and live. The program was only for a year, but I stayed behind in Florida for five more years.

I was asked to become the program director of CVIF after my year of service. God has a funny and direct way of getting my attention. Within a few short months of my new position, I was nominated to explore my vocational call to ordained ministry in an ecumenical Christian setting through the Fund for Theological Education with other young people serving in faith-based service programs from across the United States. Can you imagine my bewilderment? Certainly, there had to be a mistake! Here I was again at a faith crossroads. I began entertaining thoughts that God could use me in this world. I was nervous and I did not want to get my hopes up because the fall would be massive. I accepted the opportunity to participate in the vocational exploration program and my life is forever changed because of it. Among the esteemed staff and faith leaders, I found safe space for my authentic true self to live and thrive. I could be Black, woman, lesbian, Christian, and loved wholly. I discovered Christian denominations and houses of worship that were open and affirming. My attitude toward church changed because I knew there was a spiritual home for me where God could use me.

I moved back to Texas in 2010 to care for my aging best friend, my grandfather. However, I was not the same woman I was when I left six years prior. Healing the wounds of yesterday is an everyday practice of forgiveness and knowing each and every day God loves me just as I am. I have yet to pursue ordained ministry, but I have held the esteemed honor of mentoring and ushering other people in their vocational pursuits. I found my way back to God and she was right where I left her, in my heart.

Candace Thompson is a proud native Texan. She works as a catalyst in communities promoting transformational change by building and nurturing community leaders through the practice of generous listening, walking in solidarity, and advocating for needed changes as identified by the communities she serves. Candace earned her Bachelor of Arts in Psychology from the University of Texas at Dallas, and a dual Master's degree in Public Administration and Social Work from the University

of Texas at Arlington. Her professional and personal experiences have shaped her heart and how she moves in the world. She is a passionate social justice advocate seeking equity for all who find there is no place for them at the decision-making table. She has a heart for family (of choice and by blood), senior citizens, and youth. In her downtime, she enjoys a good book, Sufi poetry, and quality time with family and friends.

And So It Goes

Rev. Dr. Paula Stone Williams

I was never sure I believed in God. Given that I was a pastor and all, this was a problem. I had read Francis Schaeffer's *He Is There and He Is Not Silent*, which brought me closer to the holy grail of belief, but not close enough. Schaeffer worked for me because I was a thinker, not a feeler. Feelings, I had learned early, were not safe.

I was probably three or four when I knew I was a girl, yet no one treated me like the girl I knew myself to be. In the way children learn so well, I stuffed my feelings. My body appeared to be the body of a boy. Therefore, I was a boy, feelings be damned. If I could not feel my way to wholeness, I would think my way there. Hence, the problem with God. Try as you might, you cannot think yourself into belief in God.

My father was a pastor, a kind man from a theologically conservative background whose life betrayed his theology. Dad rejected no one. I took notice. My mother was, in every way, more conservative. She did not see the world as safe, and the God who created it was no exception. God was not partial to anyone's feelings, and apparently didn't have any himself, since he had passively watched his own son die and all.

Believing in God meant making sense of an Ultimate Disciplinarian who apparently did not really care if I made it to heaven. Through Bible college and seminary I fashioned some understanding of God that allowed me to enter ministry with a modicum of integrity. I never appreciated Josh McDowell's *Evidence That Demands a Verdict*, finding more convincing arguments from Francis Collins, John Polkinghorne, and Owen Gingerich. Still, there was this gnawing fear my apologetic had been created out of construction paper and did not have a prayer of withstanding a tree-bending storm.

The storm arrived when I was watching my favorite television show of all time: *LOST*. Damon Lindeloff and Carlton Cuse were the show runners. The series probed the liminal space between faith and reason, the writers playing word games with history. John Locke was not Lockean, but a man engrossed in mystery. Jack, the show's main protagonist and son of a man named Christian, was very Lockean. Jack was a Western physician, committed to science, not dwelling in the realm of mystery and faith. However, in the sixth and final season Jack came to realize Jacob (God) was real, and he had been called to sacrifice his life for the sake of his friends.

The night that show aired I was alone in my Colorado home. When Jack had his epiphany I began to wail. I wept as I had never wept before. I screamed and railed at God. "Who do you think you are to have made me this way and called me to this? I'm going to lose everything. Don't you know what this is going to do to my family?" The only sound was silence, but there was no doubt in my heart, I had been called to be Paula.

I was well known in the evangelical world, the CEO of a four-million-dollar ministry, the editor-at-large and weekly columnist of a venerable Christian magazine, a megachurch preaching pastor, and a seminary instructor. In my evangelical bubble, this was not going to go well.

When I came out on my blog (paulastonewilliams.com) there were over 65,000 page views, and most of those people were angry. I lost all of my jobs and thousands of Christian friends. I assumed my time in the church was over. It would be reasonable to assume my faith departed with my employment, but tenuous as my faith had always been, it did not abandon me. To the contrary, it transformed me.

A 2014 study by Sara Burke and Julie Bakker, two psychologists in the Netherlands, looked at the MRI results of eighty pre-hormone-treated transgender individuals. Among other findings, the scientists discovered the participants responded to an odorous steroid in the area of the hypothalamus consistent with the brains of the gender with which they identified. That was before hormone therapy. As I discovered on estrogen and anti-androgens, hormone treatment changes the brain significantly. Nowhere were the changes any more significant than in the realm of spirituality and sexuality.

Sexuality and spirituality are closely intertwined. The most common phrase repeated at sexual climax is, "Oh God!" I believe there is a reason. With estrogen and anti-androgens my sexuality and spirituality both changed massively. Since it deserves an entire chapter, or better yet, an entire book, I will save the changes in how I now experience sexuality for some later time. For now, I will focus on the spiritual changes.

I have a friend who is a camera operator in the feature film business. For years he insisted I watch *Babette's Feast*. I finally rented the film and found it did not do much for me. A few years after I became Paula I watched the film again. Oh my! The change was not in the movie. The change was in me. Paul found spirituality in proper exegesis and good hermeneutics. Paula finds spirituality in a meal with friends, in the wisdom of mothers, and in the space between human relationships. I still appreciate good exegesis and a proper hermeneutic, but spirituality is so much more.

One of my closest friends is Jen Jepsen, a woman who once knew Paul and was willing to go through the discomfort of getting to know Paula. A couple of years ago Jen began attending Highlands Church in Denver. A few months later I joined her there.

On my first Sunday I could not bring myself to go forward for communion. Jen brought the moistened bread back in her cupped hands, precious as a gift from the Magi. As I ate the bread, I knew for the second time I had been called by God. This time I was called back to the church. Within three months I was preaching at Highlands.

I do not know what to make of my newfound holistic faith. It is not important that I understand it. It is important that I experience the love of the Father, the heart-wrenching solidarity in the suffering of the Son, and the tug of the Spirit.

Jen and I are taking some big steps of faith in our neck of the woods. Shortly after what we both found to be troubling election results, Jen was in England for a conference for church planters. She was distraught, tears arriving without invitation. After one session she wrote these words:

> Day 2 (final) of the conference was remarkable! The church is in the center of Birmingham, built in 1100, freezing, but the singing! We have done traditional church choruses, and after a fitful night's sleep and the desperate need to discuss shitty Trump with a woman, God delivered, hand to heart, Paula, a miracle. The keynote speaker was Debra Green, who started Redeeming Our Communities while pregnant with her third child, birthed the movement the day the baby was born. She sat across from me (you know that church shape, the cross, stage in the middle) and watched me. I wept, wept, wept, through "In Christ Alone," particularly the part

about no life in death and resurrection and all that, didn't help that an Englishman with a lovely tenor popped in behind me. I wept and recovered barely. She gave her talk, about how God woke her up in the night with a fire in her belly, a mother of three, etc. So much my story.

Afterwards she grabbed my hand and said in the best English, "God's got a word for you. I almost called you out in my main session but it wasn't appropriate. I thought of your scarf. I was looking at it and realized my word won't require you to buy a new scarf or even to take it off. You just need to make a slight adjustment." I swear, Paula, I told her nothing of our work, no specifics. I cried and she cried and she prayed with me right there. We talked Trump and she said, "I know you are going to do something massive in the US; just looking at you, I know it."

So, if we are being prayed over by her we are going to do incredible things! I have the utmost confidence God spoke to me today through her. There is no other explanation. She God-mothered me and now I get to come home and do this work.

We are grieving and we need to grieve. It comes in waves and the men don't seem to need to—only the women and minorities. So we will. We will grieve well, we will grieve complete, we will grieve because something fundamental to who we are as a people, a nation, has died.

We can discuss the rising later; it's too soon. This is the middle Saturday. And you are amazing and fabulous and going to rise to partner with this world—when it's time.

Take care of yourself! I love you.

When I read Jen's email in my thin-walled hotel room, I was in New Jersey, speaking for a conference for parents of transgender children. As I began reading I buried my face in a hand towel and sobbed. An hour later I rose up and the towel looked like the Shroud of Turin, mascara and makeup outlining a transformed human face.

Two nights later I was back in Denver. Awakened by a dream at 4 a.m. I stared at the window, restless. I had dreamed I was at a party in which there was no food. A certain president-elect promised to find food and drove us to a fast food restaurant. When he discovered he did not have a credit card, I paid for the food. Upon returning to the house there was a woman in the living room who had not been there previously. The woman was caring for an orphan. She greeted me and said, "You are safe. I am here for you, because there is much work to do. You will be all right. I am certain." The woman had a unique look, unlike anyone I had ever seen before.

Awake and staring out the window, I tried to place the woman. Suddenly, I leapt out of bed and turned on my laptop. I searched the Internet for "Debra Green" and there she was, the woman in my dream!

Paul would have attempted a logical explanation for the visitation from Debra Green. Coincidence maybe, or possibly I had seen a picture of her in the past. Paul would have been desperate to find a rational reason for having a vivid dream about a woman I had never seen before. Paula had no such need. Call it what you will—synchronicity, the collective unconscious—I really don't care. I believe Debra Green was in my dream because the Ultimate Lover placed her there.

My life is a not easy. My loving family still must struggle with my transition. I cannot find good work that pays. Most of my old friends are gone, never to return. But I am loved by the Lord of the Universe, just as I am, and I am discovering that is enough.

If I could go back and speak to that four-year-old girl in a boy's body, I would give her this message: "This is the secret you must know. You, my precious dear, are loved by your Creator, just as you are. Now go, little girl, and life the life you were meant to live."

Rev. Dr. Paula Williams was the CEO of a large church planting organization, a megachurch preaching pastor, a magazine editor, and a seminary instructor. All ended when she transitioned from Paul to Paula. After thirty-five years in New York, Paula moved to Denver, Colorado, where she currently serves as a pastoral counselor, coach, and church consultant. She works with OPEN, a network of progressive evangelicals, coaches with the Center for Progressive Renewal, and directs the church planting team at Highlands Church in Denver. Paula also serves on the board of the Gay Christian Network and is a blogger for *The Huffington Post*. For more information visit paulastonewilliams.com.

Belonging to Myself

Billy Flood

In thinking about my sexuality and faith, I see them developing both simultaneously but separately on two different tracks. One informed the other, I guess you could say. I truly knew I was home for the holidays from undergrad when I had to trudge down into the basement and search for the big box. The one marked "Xmas" with our twenty-year-old artificial tree in it. It looked like hell unassembled. But once it was up, and my mother and I carefully unpacked the crystal, glass, and gold ornaments, we would put them on the tree while singing church carols, straight out of the Baptist hymnal. Once we got those ornaments on the tree, I felt so good inside, so warm, and for that twinkling month of December, I almost forgot my mother and father had sent me to a Christian counselor who told me I was going to hell. That silly cheap tree with the expensive ornaments made me so happy I could almost forget my mother's words, "I won't have a gay son. I just won't." Christmas isn't the same without that fake tree. I used to wonder why I had such an attachment to this plastic thing that got dressed up to be Cinderella for a month, only to go back into the basement for eleven more.

I figured out that it was emblematic that I loved a fake tree, dressed up to be something it was not. It mirrored me in some way. I was straight-acting for my parents and church at the time and gay to all of my friends, colleagues, and everyone else. I just couldn't take the straight ornaments off of me for my parents back then. But I could not hate them. They supported me in everything I did, sent me to college, paid for my car, gave me every thing I needed—but acceptance. I remember being so afraid to let them in.

As I have aged, the cavernous distance between us has eased but not become easier to traverse. Now that everything is out in the open, the truth is like a force field that separates us at times. To be frank, it is the only thing we *do not* talk about. Them both being college educated, upper middle class black people, they discuss all kinds of oppression and social justice matters. They marched and integrated lunch counters in the sixties, and even now do works of service through Greek organizations. They are charitable to all . . . except when it comes to the LGBTQ question. It is a choice for them, and always will be. Our dialogue is pleasant. The older they get the less they find the need to remind me of my damnation, and every once in a while real communication occurs and there are lovely moments of kindness, but on the whole the relationship is surface—"How is the weather?" Their resistance to my sexuality is a wall I have learned to accept and move past.

> For you created my inmost being; you knit me together in my mother's womb. I praise you because I am fearfully and wonderfully made; your works are wonderful, I know that full well. My frame was not hidden from you when I was made in the secret place. When I was woven together in the depths of the earth, your eyes saw my unformed body. All the days ordained for me were written in your book before one of them came to be. (Ps 139:13–16)

God knows me. He knows me more intimately than anyone has, ever can, or will. He knows I am gay because He knit me together.

God knows I am gay, and He loves me.

This truth, this fact that seems so simple and obvious to me now, was something hard won and a thing I anguished over for years due to the familiar clobber passages hurled down at me as a young boy from the Southern Baptist pulpit. These messages that I should hate my black and gay self comes from the media at large, and the church, especially in this time of tribalism and otherizing in the political sphere. As for my parents, I had to find a way to come to peace with them and their mind-set, because I love them and they love me, if not all of me. The way through this was to love them and simply be confident in who I am, the way God made me.

I am most interested these days in trying to build bridges with other Christians in love. Though this sounds simple, in practice it is the hardest thing I have ever done. How can I sit and listen to the words and concerns of my brother in Christ who hates me for my race and/or sexual orientation? Is this person my enemy even though we are brothers in Christ? Let me unpack that. Even if I see someone who proclaims to be a Christian shouting hate speech, is not that exactly the person who needs love? Is this not the person Jesus tells me to be kind to? "Bless those who persecute you." So it is a delicate balance of self preservation and not doing violence to myself by constantly exposing myself to violence and hate, but instead doing the hard work Jesus charged me to do, which is love in big ways.

In some ways the letter to the Corinthians is not complete. Love is patient, but it is also hard. It is kind, but it is tough. It might not envy, but it is flaming hot with passion. To put it simply, love is the most difficult thing to maintain, but easy to fall into. It is an army of contradictions marching loud and strong, yet it is the beauty we all search for. If we truly see God is love, then we can lean and live into that mystery that can sustain us in the questions. Loving often and loving hard guides me to truth and peace.

Billy Flood, MFA/AEA, is an artist, activist, and educator based in Kentucky. Investigating, exploring, and lifting up blackness is his purpose.

A Walk by the Lake

Danny Fluker

We walked along a wooded path that ran parallel to her favorite lake. This was where she came to meditate and to simply get away a bit from the demands of life as a nurse.

We'd just arrived and were taking in the scenery of the Long Leaf Pine and the cloudless, bright Carolina blue sky.

"Do you wanna sit for a bit?" she asked. There was something on her heart and she had brought me here to talk.

"No, no you are a walker, let's keep walking," she said immediately, answering her own question.

So we kept walking.

We were in a serious courtship. The kind of courtship with engagement in view.

Things were going well, or so I thought.

On that walk, she proceeded to tell me that I had done nothing wrong but she had this unspoken, deep-seated unsettling fear.

She didn't know what it was or where it came from but she believed it to be a sign from God—she couldn't go forward with the relationship.

I tried to rationalize away her fear.

I tried to convince her that fear doesn't come from God.

She was undeterred.

She didn't want to revisit this same fear six months from now, further progressed into a committed relationship.

It was best to end now on this path in the woods along the lake.

I was heartbroken.

I began to cry, the sort of cry where a single drop comes down your face. But I was successful in holding the rest.

In hindsight, I'm grateful the relationship ended and that my girlfriend trusted her gut. She had no idea I was gay and as far as I was concerned, that wasn't a reality for me either.

That was something deeply suppressed, denied, and certainly not named.

I was a man.

I was doing all the things a man was supposed to do.

I had a good job, I'd just bought my first place, and I was pursuing a woman.

That's what men do.

Especially good Christian men.

After the break-up I threw myself into work to try to ignore my pain. I even moved to another city hoping that would help.

None of it did.

When I did come to terms with my gayness (something I was deeply aware of since childhood but had never fully faced head on), it was a few years after this, through a book I'd read by a prominent author who advocated a life of celibacy for people like me. That book was a life-saver because it was the first time I'd read about other gay people of faith.

Celibacy was the answer.

I joined an online support group of other celibate gay Christians.

That was my world for the next three years.

I was also part of a local church.

I wasn't out publicly, but my pastoral leadership and close friends knew about my "struggle with same-sex attraction."

They loved and shepherded me well and stood by me in my efforts to not act out on my internal reality.

About a month after the US Supreme Court decision to legalize same-sex marriage, the pastors of my church approached me and asked if I'd be willing to speak in a video that would be part of their sermon series on human sexuality.

In the video, I'd talk about how my commitment to celibacy as a "same-sex attracted" person reflected my love for Jesus, and how according to Scripture this was the proper response for all LGBT people.

I was eager to do the video.

This would be my way of both coming out publicly and also sharing what I felt would be a helpful testimony to others.

I gratefully agreed.

The video never happened, though.

Months later, before filming, there were a number of changes happening in my life.

First, I lost my dream job.

Shortly after, I sunk into a deep funk.

Following that, I began to doubt whether what I was going to say in that video about how celibacy was the only way for all LGBT Christians to live pleasing to God, was true.

I realized that I knew nothing of affirming theology, nor did I have any affirming friendships with which to challenge my own deeply held convictions.

I threw myself into study.

I read book after book, both nonaffirming and affirming.

I also met my first gay married couple on a trip to New York while visiting family.

Affirming friendships followed as I became plugged in with local affirming gay Christians.

Slowly the posture of both my convictions and my heart began to shift. I realized that I was beginning to become compassionate toward affirming Christians, and I eventually extended that compassion toward myself.

The shift in my consciousness went from a place of viewing my queerness as dirty, broken, sinful, and alienating from God, to something whole, innate, good, beautiful, and able to be embraced and lived out.

Although I never did that video, I did come out through my blog. In a sort of cathartic release, I recounted the story of my job loss earlier on in the year and how that sent me down a path of deep study and self-reflection on the faith and sexuality question.

I made a decision to stay at my church even though they were nonaffirming. I knew I was loved well there and I also wanted to show that affirming Christians were no less Christian and could bear fruit, serve, and do all the good things good Christians were supposed to do. This lasted for about four months after I came out until I eventually had an emotional breakdown.

I realized that the part of me that I saw as wonderfully, fearfully made, a gift, purposive of God, was seen by those who loved me in my church as something sinful and to be denied.

I couldn't bear the weight of that perception.

I was crushed by the weight of my own emotions when thinking about it.

I left my church after that emotional breakdown.

I spent the next several months away from faith communities. Not for lack of affirming churches to choose from (I live in a pretty populous city), but mainly because of the emotional toll I knew investing in an entirely new group of people would take. I needed a break.

Presently, I've been out and affirming for just under a year. It's been a difficult year.

I've tried to navigate both second adolescence and the dating world, and I'm also trying to find a new faith community.

Despite the difficulty, there's nothing more rewarding than loving all of me because God loves all of me. Being authentically and wholly myself has been an unspeakably great gift of life.

Danny Fluker Jr. is an Atlanta native, IT professional, yogi, and aspiring writer. He is passionate about social advocacy, Black Boy Joy, and inspiring narratives that promote mindfulness and enoughness.

PART 3

REVIVAL

As we saw in the account of Peter in the book of Acts, the simple experience of the Spirit of God moving among a group of "unclean" individuals was all that it took to change the apostles' and elders' minds and forever change the theology of the church. The apostles could not deny the clear evidence of the Spirit's work when Cornelius and his entire household were overcome by the Holy Spirit and proclaimed their faith in Christ as Lord. What if, in our modern era, there was evidence of a similar move of the Spirit of God among a most unlikely people who are confessing their faith in Christ? Would the church be faithful to respond to the evidence of God's Spirit and move beyond a toxic, rigid theology to embrace greater inclusion and acceptance for sexual and gender minorities in the life of the church?

A 2014 Gallup poll found that nearly 53 percent of LGBT+ people identified as "moderately" to "highly religious."[1] These numbers starkly contrast the stereotypical image cast by many in modern culture that see LGBT+ people as nonreligious. In 2015, the Pew Research Center released a report that showed nearly half (48 percent) of all LGB people in the United States identified as "Christian."[2] This number had increased from

1. Frank Newport, "LGBT Population in U.S. Significantly Less Religious," *Gallup*, August 11, 2014, http://www.gallup.com/poll/174788/lgbt-population-significantly-less-religious.aspx.

2. "America's Changing Religious Landscape," *Pew Research Center*, May 12, 2015,

42 percent in 2013, and stands in stark contrast to the overall decline of Christianity among nearly every other demographic in the United States. LGBT+ Christian activist Matthew Vines responded to the report's results in a piece by Eliel Cruz in *The Advocate* magazine, saying:

> The "Christians vs. LGBT people" narrative that we hear so often is part of the story, but as the Pew poll shows, it's not all of it. In fact, it's the 48 percent of LGBT Americans who are Christians who are best positioned to change both religious attitudes about same-sex marriage and secular attitudes about religion. As LGBT Christians continue to find their voice, they'll be changing both their churches and the LGBT community for the better.[3]

Clearly, these numbers suggest that something dramatic is underway that could forever change the American religious landscape, particularly for Christians. While nearly every other demographic is declining in affiliation with Christianity, the LGBT+ demographic is slowly but consistently growing in their identification with the Christian faith. This is demonstrated not just in abstract poll numbers but also in events taking place across the country every year.

In 2016, the Gay Christian Network hosted their national conference in Pittsburgh, Pennsylvania, bringing together over three thousand LGBT+ Christians from around the world to worship, hear biblical teachings, and network with other like-minded LGBT+ people.[4]

The number of attendees has consistently grown since the first conference took place in 2003. Similarly, the Reformation Project's conferences draw hundreds of LGBT+ people together multiple times a year for intense biblical education and inclusive Christian theology.[5] In Europe, the European Forum of LGBT+ Christian Groups represents thousands of LGBT+ Christians who are working to create Christian communities that include and embrace all people, regardless of their sexual orientation or gender identity. In 2003, the Episcopal Church appointed Rev. Gene Robinson

---

http://www.pewforum.org/2015/05/12/americas-changing-religious-landscape/.

3. Eliel Cruz, "Report: Half of LGB Americans Identify As Christian," *The Advocate*, May 12, 2015, http://www.advocate.com/politics/religion/2015/05/12/report-half-lgb-americans-identify-christian.

4. Jonathan Merritt, "3 Christian Conferences, 3 Approaches to LGBT Issues," *Religion News Service*, October 27, 2016, http://religionnews.com/2014/10/27/3-christian-conferences-3-approaches-lgbt-issues/.

5. Ibid.

to be the first openly LGBT+ bishop in Episcopal history,[6] and in 2016, the United Methodist Church appointed Rev. Karen Oliveto to be the first openly LGBT+ bishop in Methodist history.[7] In 2015, I became the national spokesperson of Evangelicals for Marriage Equality, the first national, pro-marriage equality, and evangelical organization in American history,[8] representing the views of nearly 50 percent of millennial evangelicals who enthusiastically supported same-sex marriage.[9]

These numbers and examples suggest that something momentous is taking place in the church, and the fruit of this movement is good. More LGBT+ people are proclaiming their commitment to walk in the rhythms modeled by Jesus Christ. More LGBT+ leaders are rising up with inspiring visions of faithfulness, justice, and hope for the future of Christianity. More lives are being saved by the message of the unconditional love of God found in the Gospel. All of this evidence seems to suggest that what is taking place is truly a move of the Holy Spirit, and thus is a call to the church to move beyond its static doctrines and rigid interpretations of Scripture to embrace the new thing that God is doing in our day among sexual and gender minorities.

In the Book of Acts chapter 5, the apostles are arrested and put into prison by the high priest for proclaiming the Gospel of Jesus in the temple. As the apostles were brought before the high priest and the council to defend their actions, their words only "enraged" the council even more, to the point that the chief priest called for their death. Just at this moment, Gamaliel, a respected Jewish leader, stood up and said to the council:

> In the present case, I tell you, keep away from these men and let them alone; because if this plan or this undertaking is of human origin, it will fail; but if it is of God, you will not be able

---

6. Laurie Goodstein, "Openly Gay Man Is Made a Bishop," *The New York Times*, November 3, 2003, http://www.nytimes.com/2003/11/03/us/openly-gay-man-is-made-a-bishop.html.

7. Jennifer Brown, "Methodist Court Says First Openly Gay Bishop Is in Violation of Church Law, Should Face Trial," *The Denver Post*, May 10, 2017, http://www.denverpost.com/2017/04/28/gay-bishop-karen-oliveto-methodist-church/.

8. Brandan Robertson, "Evangelicals for Marriage Equality: The Story Behind Our Launch," *TIME Magazine*, September 9, 2015, http://time.com/3308983/evangelicals-for-marriage-equality-the-story-behind-our-launch/.

9. Daniel Cox and Robert Jones, "Generations at Odds: The Millennial Generation and the Future of Gay and Lesbian Rights," *Public Religion Research Institute*, August 29, 2011, https://www.prri.org/research/generations-at-odds/.

to overthrow them—in that case you may even be found fighting against God![10]

Gamaliel implored the rulers to cease their murderous pursuits against the apostles, claiming that if their work was opposed to the work of God, it would fail, and at the same time, if the apostles' work happened to be truly from God, the council would find itself working in opposition to God.

As one considers the evidence—psychological, theological, and sociological—a clear and compelling case can be made that the Holy Spirit is, in fact, doing a special work through sexual and gender minorities in the world. Yet, at the same time, opposition to the work of sexual and gender minorities has continued to grow in severity in many of the world's largest Christian denominations, only furthering the harm that is done to LGBT+ people and preventing the swift expansion of the kingdom of God. If the evidence suggests that the Holy Spirit is bringing about a revival and renewal through sexual and gender minorities, then the charge to the Christian church universally must be the same as the charge issued by Gamaliel to the council: If the work of LGBT+ inclusion is simply of "human origin," it will fail. But if it is, as I argue, a work of the Spirit of God, then not only will opposition efforts fail, but also they will posture the church against the very work of the God that we claim to serve.

Christians around the world are standing at a crossroads, and have a vitally important choice to make. Will we choose to cling to static interpretations of ancient biblical texts, rooted in a culture and system of knowledge that has been long outdated and improved upon, or will we heed the work of the Spirit of God who continues her mission to "lead us into all of the truth,"[11] calling us to explore higher ethical standards and calling us into biblical interpretations rooted in the perspective of the most vulnerable and marginalized in our midst? Though the church has consistently failed to live up to its call to be a community for the marginalized, God's work continues nonetheless. As Cheryl Anderson writes:

> If the church fails to carry out the tasks of redemption and reconciliation, that failure does not limit God's actions. . . . Marginalization is a theological point of departure. As a result, "our faith begins and ends in places of exclusion and struggle."[12]

10. Acts 5:38–39.

11. John 16:13.

12. Anderson, *Ancient Laws and Contemporary Controversies*, 170.

PART 3: REVIVAL

The call of the Spirit is now and has always been to uplift and welcome those who have been seen as "unclean" by religious groups and society. This is the example of Jesus; it is the trajectory of the ethics of the entirety of Scripture, and it is the call of the church today. Until the heterosexual members of the church are willing to sacrifice their privilege for the good of the LGBT+ community, they will continue to fail to walk in step with the Spirit of God and perpetuate a theology that brings death instead of the abundant life that the Gospel of Jesus promises to impart. But when Christians around the world recognize the good fruit being brought forth by LGBT+ people, along with the consistent draw of the Spirit toward greater inclusion, I believe we will get a profound glimpse at the world as God intends it to be, where every nation, tribe, tongue, gender, and sexual orientation stand as one in the glory of the Lord and the Spirit of Love.

In the last section of the book, we will hear stories of great hope and progress. We will hear firsthand accounts of this revival that the Holy Spirit is bringing about among LGBT+ followers of Jesus, and we will be challenged to align our lives with the flow and trajectory of this new work that God is doing in our day.

True Welcome

Candice Czubernat

A little over two years ago something completely life-changing happened that shifted my beliefs about God, myself, and the world around me. My wife gave birth to our boy/girl twins! It's a transformative experience for most people to have kids, but it was especially impactful because as a lesbian, I wasn't sure I'd ever get to be a mom. Back when I was wrestling with my attraction to women, there was no Ellen Degeneres, or out lesbian moms like Chely Wright or Cynthia Nixon; I felt like a complete oddity. The idea of being a Christian who was also a lesbian was like saying I wanted to be a unicorn, and then to say I wanted kids felt like I was asking that unicorn to have sweet baby unicorns: an impossibility! And yet what I thought was impossible, happened. I got to marry the love of my life and now we are the proud mothers to our precious Deacon and Dylan.

Becoming a parent opened up my heart in ways that I hadn't expected. One surprising change that occurred was that I began to have a desire to go back to church. So many Christians had hurt me through my process of discovering that I was gay. Going to church had become too painful of a place and so I had distanced myself from the Christian community. Even though I still very much had a close relationship with God, there were years that I didn't attend any kind of church and honestly, I hadn't planned on returning. But here I was, a mom of a little girl and boy, and all I wanted to do was be at church with them. I wanted God in their lives in a communal way. I wanted my children to experience the specialness and sacredness that happens when people come together to connect with God and one another, so I was willing to risk my past hurts so my children could have this experience.

My wife and I also wanted a place to grow in community with others, where we could find some new friends with other parents. I think if you ask any parent, this is exactly what they'd say they want in a church. In fact, when I look at my own parents' closest friends, they are all friends they made at church when my brother and I were young. These families are the people I grew up around and whom my parents still spend time with to this day. In fact, I consider many of these friends, whom my parents met at church over forty years ago, as close as family.

My wife and I also wanted a place where we could serve, as we both attended Christian colleges and seminary and had missed serving during our time away from the church. At the end of the day, I wanted a safe place to give of myself, find belonging and community, and grow in my relationship with God. And let's be honest, I was hoping to meet other parents to help me figure out how the heck to do this parenting thing.

I wasn't quite sure where to start in looking for a church, so I started Googling churches around the area that we live and to be honest, I spent the most time looking at the churches that had "cool" websites: church websites that had photos of families that looked like mine, minus the whole mommy-momma thing, but youngish parents with their children. Some of these churches talked about art, community, and Bible studies in pubs, and it all seemed like a place my wife and I could easily make friends. Point us in the direction of the Christians playing banjos and drinking microbrews and we'd easily call that place home. However, it wasn't quite that simple for us.

At this point in my story I fear you will see just how naïve I was and am. I don't want to simply sound like a whiny victim. Here's the thing, I think I was a bit naïve about finding a church as a married lesbian couple. I just thought, "Who doesn't want families to go to church?" I assumed that because we live in a place like California, churches wouldn't turn away LGBTQ people like they do in other parts of the country. I was wrong.

When I think about those few weeks while looking for a church, I remember feeling proud that we were even going to go to church. I felt proud that we were a family that wanted to do this whole church thing and that we were no longer letting our wounds get in the way. After all my research, I excitedly told my wife that I had found several churches that looked perfect for us and even though excited herself, she really hit the pause button and asked me to do one important thing—call them before we visited. It was way too vulnerable to take our kids to a place that we weren't sure was safe, or would fully welcome us as we are. Honestly, I felt scared and a part of me didn't want to call because I so badly wanted to be a part of one of these hip churches; I didn't want to have to face rejection before getting to experience them. But I wanted my wife to feel safe, so I decided to pick up the phone. I started by calling the most trendy church, as I was sure it would be cool with a lesbian couple.

Ring ring. . .

"Trendy church, this is Becky, how can I help you?"

"Yes, um, hello my name is Candice and my wife and I and our children are looking for a church and, um, I'm calling, well wondering if we are welcome to attend your church? What I mean is . . . I'm having a hard time finding the right words, but you know what I mean, will we be discriminated against, or told we are sinning as homosexuals if we come to your church?" This just might be the most awkward few sentences I've ever uttered in my life. Clearly I should have prepared my wording before that moment.

Becky quickly and anxiously spoke up, "You know, let me get someone on the phone who can talk to you."

Just so you know, if you ever need to talk to a pastor and the person answering the phones won't let you through because they are too busy to be bothered, just tell her you're gay and you get right through to the pastor. Honestly, it hadn't even occurred to me that this wasn't a question the person answering the phones couldn't just simply answer.

To say that I felt nervous was a bit of an understatement—knots filled my stomach. There I was, on hold after having just muttered the most uncomfortable questions of my life to a complete stranger and now I was going to have to say them again to whoever ended up picking the line back up. The truth is, if I hadn't wanted to go to that church as badly as I did, I would have just hung up.

I can only imagine Becky, the administrative assistant running back to the head pastor's office. "Pastor! Pastor! We have a lesbian woman on the phone wanting to know if she can come to church here! Oh god . . . oh god, I don't know what to tell her. What should I say?" Then I imagine the pastor saying in his best deep pastor tone, "I better take this one." And just then he picked up the line.

"Hello, this is Pastor Larry. How can I help you?" With the nausea that comes with being anxious looming in my body and my mind racing with all the possibilities of his response, I asked him the same question I had asked the administrative assistant.

His response was this, "You and your family are welcome to come to our church, but I don't want to mislead you. If you wanted to join our church, or serve in any way, you wouldn't be allowed. Our congregation is mixed on the subject and to my knowledge there aren't any other gay people." He followed his statement up with, "But I'd love to help you and your family find the right fit for you in the way of a church community." Even though his voice sounded kind, his words and their meaning pushed my humanity out the door. In my mind he was saying that because they consider my Christian, monogamous marriage too recklessly sinful, we weren't welcome to be a part of their community just like every other person who walks through the doors of their church is. We were excluded and perhaps he thought if he said it in a nice enough tone, I wouldn't feel the punch to my gut.

He mentioned a few churches that were "super liberal" and "inclusive of all," but I had already found that they didn't have young families like ours in attendance, or were a minimum of an hour away from where we lived. So I said to him, "We want to come to a church like yours where the worship is contemporary and where we'll find other families with kids our kids' age. These churches you mention are filled with mostly older people. What should we do?"

The pastor was silent for a moment and then followed up with, "Yeah, I guess you're right. Hmmm . . ." And then more silence. At that point I knew the conversation was over.

I called two more churches and I'm not exaggerating when I say this, but all three pastors said the same exact thing and in almost the exact same tone. It was so eerie and similar that I almost wondered if they all went to the same training on "how to reject a homosexual while sounding super nice about it." These conversations felt like someone had ripped my heart out. I was shocked and angry.

My wife got home from work that evening and in my hurt, as I told her what had happened using some choice words, I declared we were never going back to church. In my anger, I hated the church and I hated Christianity. Well, it didn't take much for her to soften my heart. As she gently took my hand and asked how I really felt, my anger turned to sadness and I began to weep. She held me until there were no more tears to cry. I get teary just thinking about it now. My hopeful, naïve heart was not prepared to be so blatantly rejected.

The thing is, the pastor had made a suggestion of where to try, and I quote, "Well, hmm, um, there is a place, but um, well they are very liberal. I mean they are really out there on some issues and I just don't know what to think about it. But I know there are other gay people there and I believe you're welcome to serve and be members there as a gay person."

We had heard of this particular church but had wanted something smaller and, for lack of a better word, evangelical, but we decided to give it a try. I will never forget the feelings of excitement, fear, and anxiety as we entered the church that day. Even though I knew this church was safe I felt fearful because of the hurt other churches caused. This church is Episcopal and so the beginning of the service opens with a procession. As the music began to play and the congregation began to sing, and as our kids saw the flags wave and the robed choir and staff walk down the center of the church, they began to bounce and a look of wonder came over their faces. It was like my kids were feeling the openness in this new environment, the healing and Spirit of God that was ours in a church that welcomed our family fully as we are. They weren't old enough to have words for it, but somehow I think they felt it. As I stood there that day I began to cry. With tears in my eyes, I looked over at my wife and she was crying too. We were safe to be a family, safe to worship, and safe to be at church. We had found our home.

This church is now our family and we have built the friendship-community with other parents like we hoped. I'm not sure I've ever been in a service where my heart has been so changed by the Spirit of God through what is preached from up front. I'm so grateful that this is our church; I wouldn't have it any other way. I cry every single time when they say from the pulpit that I, as a person who is part of the LGBTQ community, am just as much a part of the body of Christ and that I am beautiful just as I am. That message to my soul will never get old.

Candice Czubernat is a writer, speaker, and licensed therapist. She's also a married lesbian, Christian woman, and mother of twins. She's the founder of the Christian Closet, a web-based counseling practice where she specializes in seeing those needing a safe place to reconcile their faith with their sexual and gender identities. She has been in the mental health field for over a decade and has used her expertise in her book *The First 90 Days*, a devotional resource for parents that walks them through the first three months of their child coming out. *The Advocate* magazine named

her one of the "10 Pro-LGBT Religious Women You Should Know." If you want to read more of her story, she writes about it on her blog at candiceczubernat.wordpress.com. You can also find out more about her therapy practice at www.thechristiancloset.com.

I Am a Son of God

Andrew Deeb

Identified as male from the time I could talk. It wasn't until elementary school that I fully realized I wouldn't wake up one morning with my body reflecting my identity. I didn't have a word for what I was until eighth grade. I tried to come out in tenth grade. My parents weren't supportive, to say the least, so I dropped it. My senior year of high school I realized I needed to transition in order to keep living. I had always known, but I didn't want to face it. I slowly started coming out when I was eighteen. I lost a number of close friends, some claiming that God hated people like me or that I was going down a dangerous path. I was ostracized and outed to those I wasn't ready to tell. Some people from my former youth group have since admitted that they were trying to get me to kill myself. I publicly came out and began transitioning when I was twenty. Shortly before coming out I was walking to class and thinking about the possibility of transitioning. I went to a private Christian college and wasn't sure what the future held. I prayed, "God, I can't do this unless you are with me." Immediately I was overwhelmed by a sense of peace and an undeniable sense of the presence of God. Even though my attendance was infrequent in the months leading up to my coming out, I was concerned that my church would not accept me. I talked to one of the pastors before publicly coming out, offering to leave the church. He assured me that I was still welcome and my church became a large part of my support system.

Likewise, much to my surprise, I wasn't kicked out of the college I was attending. They requested that I move off campus for the first year while they sorted out how to handle transgender housing. It wasn't ideal. I wasn't allowed to have a roommate and was very isolated. A representative from the student life office insisted on meeting with me every so often. I agreed and raised my concerns about my isolation and voiced a desire to move on campus. It was denied. Furthermore, I wasn't allowed to visit the dorm of either gender except for limited hours on certain days of the week. The representative also made comments about what bathroom I used and said something along the lines of, "It would be safer for everyone if you didn't use the bathrooms on campus." I ended up filing a complaint with the Department of Education, prompting the school to request a Title IX exemption. The school then modified their policies to include language that excludes transgender people from campus facilities and gives the school the right to expel gender nonconforming students. All of this was done to reflect "Christ-like values."

During this process I began to discern a call toward ministry. I began looking into the process of getting ordained with the denomination I grew up in—the Lutheran Church Missouri Synod (LCMS). Initially, they seemed okay with ordaining a trans person, as long as I remained celibate. Someone from one of the LCMS seminaries said that my gender identity wouldn't be a problem, so I transferred to an LCMS college in order to prepare for seminary. As I was finalizing my transfer, I was informed that someone higher up in the denomination decided they couldn't ordain "people like me." Shortly after that, my church decided that they didn't want to support my transition after all. The church elders served me a letter stating that in order to remain an active part of the church I had to agree to remain celibate, not use the gendered bathroom in the church building, and submit to "special discipleship meetings" with the elders. They cited a number of Bible verses to support their objections. I tried to meet their demands at first, but decided I had enough after walking a half mile to a McDonald's to use a bathroom. I left the church, and the pastor has since told the congregation that I am living in unrepentant sin.

A month or so after that I went in for bottom surgery. It went poorly. A few days after the initial surgery I was rushed back into the operating room with internal bleeding. Additionally, there was a malfunction with my morphine pump and I received a near fatal dosage of morphine. As if that wasn't enough, I contracted an infection in the hospital that turned septic. It was during this time that I began to believe the things that my former church had said—that it was sinful to be the way I was and God was punishing me for being transgender.

The year following was one of the darkest of my life. I believed God to be uncaring or angry and vengeful. Whatever the case, I wanted nothing to do with Him. I couldn't really run from God or the church. I was still in college finishing up a degree in theology and biblical languages. My classwork forced me into the Bible every day and I eventually found my faith again.

I am now in seminary working toward an Mdiv and an MA in Systematic Theology. My current research is centered around the concepts of inner and outer person in the writings of Paul and how they may apply to transgender individuals. My studies have led me to the conclusion that the Bible does not talk about transgender people. There are instances of gender nonconforming individuals in Scripture, but none of them can be properly equated to transgender individuals. The verses the conservative church uses to exclude transgender people are being taken out of context and utilized in a manner that they were never intended. The rhetoric of nonaffirming churches communicates that God created and declared all things good, except for LGBT+ individuals. Denying a transgender person the ability to transition is denying that person access to God. As Søren Kierkegaard says, "The self connects with the power which created it in order to arrive at the true self. One must first know and embrace themselves before they are able to connect that self to any other force."

My personal faith has recovered some, but I still have a lot of healing to do. Christian groups and establishments have treated me more like a problem than a person. I struggle to believe that I have a place in the church. Despite this, I have found love and acceptance in Christ. God was the first to confirm my identity as male by calling me His son. There is freedom for LGBT+ individuals in the Gospel. The Gospel of Christ is one of radical love and inclusion. The Gospel is unconcerned with drawing lines of who is in and who is out, but rather shows that we are all the same—we are all sinners made saints by the blood of Christ.

Andrew (Andy) Deeb grew up in Ann Arbor, Michigan. He currently is an Mdiv student at San Francisco Theological Seminary. Andy graduated from Concordia University Ann Arbor in 2016 with a degree in pre-seminary studies/theological languages. Andy is the music minister at Gathering Desire, a Disciples of Christ congregation in San Anselmo, California.

Spiritual Life Unleashed

Minister Winner Laws

As a pre-teen growing up in Houston, Texas, the "buckle" of the Bible belt, I recognized early on that I liked girls in a way that was not accepted by society, especially the Black church. I was baptized in a Black Southern Baptist church. Family and church were key foundation blocks of validation for my emotional well-being, positive mental health, and spiritual growth. These human developmental activities impacted my self-confidence, relationship development, and theological belief systems as I evolved from a pre-teen, unsure of my sexual orientation, to a confident woman ready to enlighten the conservative Black church community about God's unconditional love for Black LGBTQ persons.

In Junior High School, I was verbally bullied by my seventh grade classmates when I once asked to carry a girl's books home for her after school. I actually had no idea what the words "dyke" or "lesbian" meant until I looked them up in a dictionary. I was so ashamed I changed schools. I was emotionally distraught, but more so afraid my parents and friends would find out about my attraction to girls. I felt I was doing something wrong, even vile based on the definitions in the dictionary.

Messages from Black conservative preachers proselytizing "I was an abomination" and that I was "unnatural" resonated loudly. Based upon their interpretation of some biblical Scriptures, they disqualified me from God's love. They called out specific verses in Leviticus, Romans, 1 Timothy, or 1 Corinthians to substantiate their rhetoric of exclusion. It was almost impossible for an LGBTQ person like me to believe that God loves unconditionally when a preacher ostracizes in word and in deed because of a person's sexual orientation. Ministers are responsible for shaping an individual's spirituality, but instead of fostering unconditional love, they used their traditional interpretation of the Bible to directly separate God's love from LGBTQ people by putting limitations and conditions on it.

I was attracted to several girls throughout high school and college; however, I dated men because it was socially and religiously acceptable. I was engaged to be married to a man for three and a half years. He called the engagement off following our graduation. I was sincerely heartbroken but it was for the best.

Deep in my soul I knew I needed to reconcile spiritually my feelings for women, so I sought to find hope in the Bible. I searched to find Scripture that communicated that I too was accepted by God. It was desperately important to find Scripture that expressed God's love for me.

I knew how I felt physically and emotionally when I was in a relationship with a man versus a woman. The Black church I grew up in taught me that being with a man was the "right thing to do"; however, I knew that when I was with a woman I felt it was the right thing for me to do. It felt natural to be with a woman. These natural feelings, with my growing understanding of God's unconditional love, compelled me to want preachers, pastors, priests, leaders, and congregants to interpret Scripture with grace and without limitations, not just for me but for all LGBTQ individuals in the church, home, and community.

I never heard the "unconditional love message" from the pulpit as it related to the LGBTQ people until I visited the Cathedral of Hope (CoH) in Dallas, Texas. The church's pastor, Rev. Michael Piazza, preached on the topic of "Holy Homosexual." When I heard this message and others like it each Sunday, I began to resolve the disconnect between my spiritual upbringing at my home church in Houston and my theological understanding based on my strong faith, which reaffirmed that God accepts us all.

Although the worship service was completely different than the Black church worship experience, I heard the Holy Spirit every time I attended CoH. I felt loved unconditionally and accepted as a Black lesbian, truly belonging to God's family through Jesus' sacrifice.

Initially, I was a tortured and wandering soul, unable to share my life explicitly with my church, family, and circle of heterosexual friends. During my personal studies, I came to know that there were three primary theological issues paramount to the spiritual life of the Black LGBTQ. They are love, inclusion, and acceptance. From a hermeneutical perspective, there are several Scriptures in the New Testament that discuss inclusion, acceptance, and love for all. Two specific Scriptures are 1 Pet 2:9: "But you are a chosen race, a royal priesthood, a holy nation, God's own people in order that you may proclaim the mighty acts of him who called you out of darkness into his marvelous light." The second is Matt 5:47: "And if you greet only your brothers and sisters, what more are you than doing than others? Do not even the Gentiles do the same?"

In reconciling homosexuality and Christianity, I read and studied Jesus' life. Throughout His entire ministry, He dealt with outcasts, adulterers, Pharisees, and tax collectors. The core of Jesus' actions exhibited the classic model of generosity, compassion, empathy, and the expression of unconditional love for the oppressed. How can preachers today espouse that they are like Jesus and believe in Jesus if their actions demonstrate that they deny and pass judgment on people because of their sexual orientation?

It was imperative for me to learn as much as I could about the Bible so I could share with others the Good News I was learning at CoH. My personal relationship with God had been enhanced and my confidence level grew to the extent that I was being invited to speak at people's homes and churches. I shared affirming answers to questions like, "Does God love me?" and "What is the true meaning behind the 'clobber passages?'" Once I read the book *God and the Gay Christian* by Matthew Vines, I had a better understanding of why and how these passages were used to denounce LGBTQ people and their relationships. The book provided enlightening facts such as, "Prior to 1869, terms meaning 'homosexual' and 'homosexuality' didn't exist in any language, and they weren't translated in English until 1892."[1] Key truths like the aforementioned one are relevant to giving all of the information to people attempting to determine if LGBTQ persons are loved by God unconditionally.

My personal commitment to learn more about God evolved as a result of my experiences attending CoH. I felt compelled to advance my knowledge through a theological education at Brite Divinity School in Fort Worth, Texas. The more knowledge I gained through my studies, the more it validated that God loves me just as I am. God created me as a Black lesbian and loves me unconditionally, just like the blind man in John 9:1–3. Jesus' miracle was a metaphorical message to all who saw him heal the blind man. People are blind and in the dark until they open their mind and souls to God.

1. Matthew Vines, *God and the Gay Christian: The Biblical Case in Support of Same-Sex Relationships* (New York: Convergent, 2003) 161.

Another key Scripture I studied was Ps 139:14. It states that God made us and knows exactly who we are before birth. There is nothing God does not know about who I am because the Creator is omnipresent and omniscient. It is reassuring that God knows everything about us and is with us no matter where we are—physically, spiritually, or emotionally.

There is a correlation between these Scriptures (Ps 139:14 and John 9:1–3) that deserves further dialogue. They both share that God knows who we are before our birth, at our birth, and after our birth. There are no mistakes. God created each of us and understands our gifts, our imperfections, and our purpose. These Scriptures liberated me to be the best Winner Laws I can be. I believe that it benefits both straight and LGBTQ individuals to study the Bible and discover the Scriptures that can release them from the dogmatic theological viewpoints of excluding LGBTQ from the love of God.

The blog *God Made Me Gay* comprises information that is highly recommended for any religious zealot or anyone concerned about God's love for an LGBTQ person. It specifically contains an article titled, "A Letter to Louise: A Biblical Affirmation of Homosexuality," which was written by a pastor to one of his congregants addressing the Scriptures that preachers use in their sermons to condemn LGBTQ people.[2]

If people of faith became better equipped to state their own theological viewpoints of inclusivity for all people, an ecumenical movement could emerge and unite all people regardless of their sexual orientation. The investment of energy and effort to learn more about God's unconditional love is worth the effort.

It is time to deconstruct biblical myths and help others interpret Scripture to find love and inclusion for all. LGBTQ people of all races deserve to live their lives without others imposing their unwarranted opinions regarding their sexuality. No one should have to fear who they are. I learned this personally by studying multiple versions of the Bible. Scripture has multiple contexts including historical, biblical, literal, and cultural. It was an eye-opening revelation to learn that there are more than two hundred versions of the Bible. The book *What the Bible Really Says About Homosexuality* by Daniel Helminiak shares the benefits and liabilities of reading the Bible from a literal approach and a historical-critical approach, which could lead to misinterpretation of God's love for LGBTQ individuals.

2. Bruce Lowe, "A Letter to Louise: A Biblical Affirmation of Homosexuality," *God Made Me Gay* (blog), http://godmademegay.blogspot.com/p/letter-to-louise.html.

The propensity for the traditional Black church and Black families to continue ostracizing, discriminating, and denouncing Black lesbians and other LGBTQ people is unacceptable in the eyes of God. Horace L. Griffin, in his book *Their Own Receive Them Not: African American Lesbians & Gays in Black Churches*, validates that Black LGBTQ persons should not have to exchange their culture, family, and background to feel and know God's love in the Black church. I would expect the level of acceptance to increase once people have the theological understanding that is commensurate with Jesus Christ's teaching and God's will. Unconditional love is the only way for us to achieve the epitome of God's extravagant grace. I know now through prayer and meditation why I am called to facilitate better interdependent relationships as a light for all of God's children to know the loving, nurturing, forgiving, and gracious Creator of the Universe.

I know that God led me to Brite Divinity School to gain a theological education and to offer hope to others like myself. It requires courage, faith, and tenacity to dig deep, listen, and hear the Holy Spirit calling one to a greater purpose. As a Black lesbian, I understand that without hope there is despair, and without faith there is uncertainty. I know God wants me to share my faith, my theology, and my life with others, including straight people, as a testimony that He lives in us and to give them all hope.

As I progress in my calling with my spiritual life unleashed, I will continue to serve God and experience the joy of living in this body as a Black lesbian, knowing that God made me and loves me unconditionally.

Minister Winner Laws is spiritually called to make a difference in the lives of others through her gifts and talents. Since 2000, she has been a member of Cathedral of Hope (CoH) UCC. She has been a leader of multiple CoH ministries and served on the Board of Stewards from 2003 to 2006. She is working with CoH to have a spiritual space that welcomes Black LGBTQ persons. Black LGBTQ people have unique spiritual perspectives as a result of their lived church experiences. She wants them to know that God loves them unconditionally. Businesses and church organizations have benefited from her leadership, project management, and teamwork skills. Originally from Houston, she currently resides in Plano, Texas. She earned a Master of Theological Studies from Brite Divinity at Texas Christian University. Her passions include faith development, leadership, family, and golf.

Who Owns God?

Christopher Arlen

H ere's the question: Who owns God?
One of the great luxuries of time is the ability to stand in future
age and look back and reflect on our collective past. When we look back
today it is easy to clearly see many of the great injustices that have been
committed in the name in Christianity, the church, or God himself. From
our present vantage point, we see the church's historic struggle with inclusion and acceptance — from the first century through today.

If I were to stand before you and share with you some of the great
intellectual thoughts and writings of some of the religious and cultural
thought-leaders of 1864, the vast majority of you would likely be stunned
into silence by the ignorant and hate-laced words. Words penned by Christian men who held, in faith, faulty notions of white superiority and the so-
called "inferior races." Hopefully you, like me, would today consider these
ideas to be un-Christian, un-American, and woefully unholy.

For slaveholders, Christianity not only justified slavery, it was em-
ployed as a means of control used to religiously subdue their slaves. Slaves
were taught to obey their masters with fear and trembling—as they would
fear God. God, Himself, they believed, had decreed, established, and
blessed the institution of slavery.

Many slaveholders viewed themselves to be good and upright Christian men. Some, even though they found themselves afflicted with moral unease about slavery, accepted that slavery was ordained by God.

One leading Bishop of the day wrote:

> If it were a matter to be determined by personal sympathies, tastes, or feelings, I should be as ready as many man to condemn the institution of slavery, for all my prejudices of education, habit, and social position stand entirely opposed to it. But as a Christian, I am solemnly warned to be "wise in my own conceit," and not to "lean on my own understanding."[1]

Like many today, when it comes to LGBT issues within the church, this bishop found himself torn between the rational humanity of conscience and the irrational orthodoxy of literalism. His personal dislike of slavery was in conflict with what he viewed as the plain sense of the Bible. The biblicism of the proslavery movement rendered rational judgment in the debate over moral issues a form of religious infidelity.

In fact, the Southern Baptist Convention, the second largest denomination in the United States and the denomination in which I was raised, was formed specifically to defend the cruel and un-Christian institution of slavery. Looking back, it is clear to see—thankfully—that these attitudes, while seemingly justified by Scripture, were patently false and based in personal and social prejudices along with the religious ignorance of the age.

Likewise, Christianity was invoked against women in the 1900s to subjugate and control their place in society. And if I were to share some of the prevailing thoughts of the age about women, I'm sure you would likewise be appalled.

Think about it: at the beginning of the twentieth century, women were outsiders to the political system—unable to serve on juries, unable to vote, and deemed patently unqualified to hold elective office.

A woman had no legal identity of her own—she was simply an extension of her husband. His identity was hers. She had no rights when it came to consent or reproduction. She could hold no property of her own. She was unable to pursue the career of her choice. The Supreme Court even

---

1. The Rt. Rev. John Henry Hopkins, Bishop of Vermont and Presiding Bishop of the Episcopal Church, writing in 1861 in *A Scriptural, Ecclesiastical, and Historical View of Slavery, from the Days of the Patriarch Abraham to the Nineteenth Century* (New York: Pooley & Co., 1864) 5–12.

once ruled that women were not considered persons under the Fourteenth Amendment to the Constitution.

Many in the church used the Bible to subdue and control women. As women struggled for their rights, arguments about nature and social order were used to undermine nearly every attempt to improve the standing of women. Scripture held, they falsely believed at the time, that a woman's place was in the home—taking care of her man and her family—certainly not as an engaged citizen.

Judge these words for yourself. "The appropriate duties and influence of woman are stated in the New Testament. . . . The power of woman is in her dependence, flowing from the consciousness of the weakness which God has given her for her protection. . . . When she assumes the place and tone of man as a public reformer, she yields the power which God has given her—and her character becomes unnatural."

Both the abolition of slavery and the inclusion and empowerment of women in society were at one time considered to be atheistic pursuits. Abolitionists who were Christian were condemned as heretics or infidels. Those Christians who supported the Woman's Suffrage Movement were viewed as apostates—abandoning the love of God and the fellowship of mainstream Christianity.

Even closer to the present age, one can view the landmark civil rights case *Loving v. Virginia*. Mildred and Richard Loving were a young interracial couple. They were not activists, nor were they seeking to lead or be part of a movement—they were simply a man and woman who fell in love and wanted to spend their lives together as man and wife.

In the early half of this century, the Christian Church played an unfortunate role in stigmatizing interracial marriage in the United States. White supremacy and "racial purity" were justified by stereotyping interracial unions as sexually perverted and sinful—especially for "good" white Christians. If a white Christian man were to look upon a black woman with interest, he was taught that the wrongness of his action would immediately seize him and convict him in his spirit.

In 1958, the Lovings found themselves awakened in the bedroom of their house by the police. They had violated the Virginia Racial Integrity Act of 1924, which forbade interracial marriage. Faced with prison, the Lovings were forced to leave the State of Virginia for a period of twenty-five years. When they could no longer tolerate being away from their families, their friends, and their support systems, they returned to Virginia and were arrested.

The trial judge, with his own biases and convictions, invoked the religious ignorance and prejudices of the age when we wrote in his opinion, "Almighty God created the races white, black, yellow, malay and red, and he placed them on separate continents. And but for the interference with this arrangement there would be no cause for such marriages. The fact that he separated the races shows that he did not intend for the races to mix." Fortunately, this arcane and wrong-headed ruling was overturned by the Supreme Court in 1967.

When the Court heard *Loving v. Virginia*, the justices voted unanimously to strike down the Virginia law, with Chief Justice Warren writing that "the freedom to marry has long be recognized as one of the vital personal rights essential to the orderly pursuit of happiness by free men." This landmark ruling led to the overturning of miscegenation laws in fifteen states. This precedent also factored into the recent marriage equality ruling.

So from my perspective, looking through the long lens of time—racist, sexist, and bigoted attitudes born of Christianity have been the norm. I have been gay for as long as I have been Black—the two are intertwined in my spirit, my heart, and my psyche.

This is my testimony and my witness: each of us bear the great privilege and responsibility for finding God for him or herself. Throughout history, there has existed the need for humankind to find new ways to know and experience God. In the Baptist tradition, we refer to this a Soul Liberty—which is to say that we embrace a deep conviction that every man or woman can enter into direct relationship with God without any outside mediation.

Standing at the intersection of race, sexuality, and faith, I can do no other than to trust the eternality of my spirit to God. I cannot accept what has been said about Black people and race in the name of God and still love Jesus as my savior. I cannot subjugate and objectify women because God somehow planned for this as the "natural order." Nor can I absolutely not love my biracial nephews, my white brother-in-law, my white husband, or the many interracial couples who have cultivated loving relationships based on trust, integrity, and mutuality.

But God is faithful. In every age, it seems, God has sent pioneering way-showers to help restless societies understand and address the challenges of the age—bold outliers who stand in the gap to bridge social issues, religious practice, and individual freedom. Theologies of liberation become necessary to see and celebrate God's unfolding plan for us all. History teaches us that our understanding of those who are different is always be evolving.

Our shameful history and the attitudes that supported the sinful institution of slavery continued on through the civil rights movement and continues today as evidenced by the necessity of the Black Lives Matter movement. Attitudes toward women and their role in society have also evolved, yet we still fight for a woman's right to exercise agency over her own body. Women still make less than men for the same work. And, I can attest to the fact that interracial relationships still raise the occasional sideways glare. But we *have* moved forward.

In time, I am convinced that those who come after us will look back and at our age and judge our current struggle for LGBT inclusion, to be able to worship openly and honestly as we live lives of wholeness and integrity. I am hopeful that they will judge us well as we are being called to be the pioneering witnesses of our day—standing at the gate, welcoming the prodigals as they make their long way home.

So the question was this: Who owns God? The answer is simple and true: God belongs to all of us.

Christopher Arlen is a minister, an advocate for gay men's health, and a powerful voice for spiritual liberation. Embracing a philosophy of wholeness rather than pathology, he has worked with gay men's communities in Los Angeles, San Francisco, and San Diego, California, as well as Tucson, Arizona, and here in Colorado. Raised in the Southern Baptist tradition, Christopher has served as youth minister, worship leader, evangelist, and summer missionary. For a short time as a young adult, he had a wife. Christopher left Christian ministry in 1988. In 1991, Christopher took up the cause of HIV prevention and LGBT civil rights. Providing critical testimony for the Riverside Coalition Against Discrimination, Christopher began to understand and play at the dynamic intersection of faith and sexuality. He later served as Southern California Co-Chair for Civil Rights for the L.I.F.E. Lobby (Lobby for Individual Freedom and Equality). Trained as a community health outreach worker, Christopher has worked with gay men in a myriad of spaces—within high-risk environments, within community spaces, and within the church. He has developed successful programs for the National Task Force on AIDS Prevention, the National Black Lesbian and Gay Leadership Forum, San Francisco's acclaimed Glide Memorial Church, and a host of others. Christopher is principal consultant for the Soft Skills Company, working

with organizations to foster positive relational dynamics through facilitation, mediation, and skills-based training programs. He is also principal mediator at Arlen Dispute Resolution Services, where he employs his extensive experience bringing people together to explore and discover new paths to move past life's unexpected upsets. He currently serves as membership chair at First Baptist Church of Denver. He lives in Lakewood with his husband, Damon, and their two dogs, Oliver and Sofia.

Do Not Wait

A Benediction

Matthew David Morris

Do not wait until it makes sense to love me.
Love me now.
Love me fearlessly.
Love me in spite of your nonbelief.
Do this, and you will know what it feels like
to be loved by the one who made and who adores you.
Do this, and you will walk the path of
The One who showed us that death is not the end of love.
Do this, and the Love which gave birth to all being,
The Love which resides deep within your own self,
will pour forth from your lips like rain,
nourishing the earth
and healing the wounds
inflicted upon us
all.
But do not wait.
Love me now.

We are each home to a small piece of the Holy. God's love is fierce, and we are called to join God in that sacred fierceness.

God will not be cast out. It simply cannot be done. Our hearts are already occupied, as is this world. The holy fire of God burns as brightly now as it ever has. Pentecost is a perpetual flame that burns within the hearts of God's children. The God who ignites this fire in you, inspiring you to lift your arms in praise, is the same God that moves me to dance, to sing along with Aretha and Whitney, to transgress the cultural expectations that have been placed upon us both.

God transgresses culture at every turn. Amen?

God is bigger than our institutions; bigger than our best attempts at goodness.

And I welcome God into my heart. This God who was, and is, and will be Love Incarnate is no more absent from my heart than my heart is absent from my chest. I welcome God in again and again, and I will do so as many times as it takes for it to be known that God was always already there.

I welcome God into my heart through my kindness and compassion. I welcome God into my heart by witnessing to the movement of God's Spirit through this world. I welcome God into my heart when I dance and celebrate the gift of this flesh, formed inside the body of a woman. I welcome God into my heart each time I proclaim that the kingdom of God that Jesus so persistently described is in fact a *kin-dom*; one in which we are *all* God's beloved. This kin-dom is so thoroughly permeated with an awareness of God's presence and love that it becomes unthinkable to cast a person out; for to cast out one of God's creation is to cast out the Creator, and the Creator cannot be cast out.

So, neither should we cast out those who the Creator claims as beloved.

A church that does not love and look to the witness of those living on the margins is a Church of Nonbelief. Christians become nonbelievers the moment we assume that God is not already animating and illuminating the lives of the outcast. We become nonbelievers the instant we judge one of God's children as worthless. We become nonbelievers when we lock a person out of our communities for the sake of our own piety. As one who has seen the church from both inside and out, I can testify to this. It can feel barren on the outside. Desert-like.

But God moves through the desert, too. There is no place where God is not present. God is moving in the club. God is speaking through the Drag Queen. God is changing lives in ways that Sunday Morning Christians don't even realize. God raises the dead as quickly as we execute them, because the love of God is stronger than any violence we can inflict upon one another.

God's love is paramount.

And this is the point I'm trying to make: none of us have a monopoly on God. We cannot claim God as our own at the exclusion of another person. It's simply not possible. God is infinitely more generous than we are. When we pull back, God moves forward. When we refrain, God indulges. We articulate our conditions; God offers eternal life. God cares nothing for our religious posturing. God, through Jesus, asks only two things of us:

Love one another, and love God.

Period.

End of story.

Done.

Finished.

That's. It.

Love God so much that you don't have to question whether or not to love me.

Love me so much that you don't have to wonder whether or not you love God.

Love with an abandon that can birth the universe.

Love with a generosity that can raise the dead.

Love with a relentlessness that can save the nations.

Love beyond your doubt, your fear, your anxiety, and your pain.

And in the moment that you think you should judge, love.

In the moment you lean toward unkindness, love.

In the moment when you listen back to that one sermon you heard, when the preacher sewed a seed of doubt in your mind about whether or not I was worthy of your love, suggesting to you that perhaps loving should feel more like suspicion, or unbelief, or distrust . . .

Love.

Do not listen to the voices that suggest there is another viable option besides love.

Do not listen to the pundits that encourage anything other than love as a viable platform.

Do not proclaim anything other than love, because you and I are made of love, as was Jesus.

And if we are to follow in the footsteps of the Savior, we better get used to the feeling of love in our bodies. We better get so practiced in this love that when Jesus returns he will instantly recognize that the world that

we have helped to cultivate is the same world that he described some two
thousand years ago.

> Love is happening. Right now.
> Get on board. Do not wait.
> Love me.
> I am your neighbor.
> God made me, just as God made you.
> Love me for the sake of your own salvation.
> Love me because the end is coming, and it is already here, and there is no
> better moment to love than the present.
> Let God into you heart.
> Remember where you came from: Love is the origin.
> Love, sacrificed in a world hungry for power, is resurrected
> for the purpose of proclaiming the truth about itself:
> Love was, and is, and continues to be.
> Love God through me.
> Love me, and in so doing, love God.
> Love me in order that you might be more like Jesus.
> Do it now.
> Do now wait.
> Love me, just as God loves you.

**Matthew David Morris is a student of theology, an internationally re-
nowned musician and performer, and a Grammy-nominated songwriter
living in Portland, Oregon, with his husband and their family. He ministers in a number of capacities within and among the churches of the Episcopal Diocese of Oregon, and he is engaged in local activism for people
experiencing homelessness and marginalization. He spent several years
engaged in the contemporary Neopagan community, and his current
theological work centers around a belief that the God of the Christian
faith is a God of liberative love, whose love extends to all creation. Part
storyteller, part songwriter, part critical philosopher and theologian,
Matthew David's words aim to lay bare with poetic care the harder truths
of our day. More of his writing can be found at matthewdavidmorris.com.**

Conclusion

An Invitation

Brandan Robertson

In these pages, you have read the stories of struggle, pain, faith, and love that make up the experience of so many LGBT+ Christians from every walk of life and background. You have read about the many ways that the body of Christ has failed us and harmed us. You have read of our resiliency and faithfulness even in the midst of the most severe persecution and oppression. You have read of our vision for the future, of a church and a world where all are welcomed to boldly step into their place at the table of God's grace.

Now the question you must ask yourself is this: *What now will you do?*

Will you put this book on the shelf and go back to living life as you were before you spent time with these stories? Or will you take a step forward, moving toward the Holy Spirit's call to inclusion, liberation, and love? Whether you are an LGBT+ person, an ally, or a nonaffirming Christian, it is my sincere hope that you have been challenged by these stories and the faithful witness of every life contained in these pages. I hope that you are provoked to take the next right move, whether toward coming out and embracing your God-created identity, or seeking to uplift the voice of LGBT+ people in your faith community, or repenting of the harm that has been done by the church and taking tangible steps to change the way the church teaches about LGBT+ people.

Whatever you do, you now have heard the voices and seen the lives of this great cloud of queer witnesses, and I hope that you will carry us with you in your heart and mind in the coming days. I hope that our stories bring about conviction and hope, restlessness and peace, sorrow that turns to joy. Because the Holy Spirit of God is doing a new thing in the church and the world through the lives of LGBT+ individuals, and this movement cannot be stopped. It is my prayer that this book serves as an invitation to you to join with us in the amazing work that God is doing, and that you will join us as the kingdom of God is manifest all the more powerfully on earth as in heaven through us.

This is our witness.

Afterword

Bishop Joseph Tolton

My Presiding Bishop, Rev. Dr. Yvette Flunder, is convinced that Christianity is due for a new testament. After reading the compelling and courageous stories compiled in *Our Witness* I am reminded of the shift happening in the body of Christ as queer people of faith find our footing and claim our rightful place in the kingdom of God. Nelson Mandela said, "Revolution without reconciliation is not revolution [it is merely an exchange of power]." As students of radical inclusivity we are properly taught to be the church and not try to change the church. As I grow in grace I realize that by being the church, in fact we are changing the church. I am clear that not all people of faith will become affirming, but I bid you to consider the breadth and scope of what God has called us to impact.

I am proud to serve the Fellowship of Affirming Ministries as the Bishop of Global Ministries. The focus of my work is being an ambassador of goodwill to LGBTI communities in hostile climates in Africa, Asia, and the Caribbean. I am amazed by the move of God among people who risk their very lives to gather in worship, who live perpetually in peril of anti-gay sentiment manifesting itself in violence or social dislocation. I am often asked what brings me back to Uganda time and time again? What motivates my consistent response to pastoral care needs in dicey contexts? Why am I so committed to breaking ground in spiritual environments so committed to defeating me?

My secular vocation is advertising, and owning my own creative boutique has kept me focused on the bottom line. My ability to stay solvent and ultimately profitable is based on developing communications that drive my client's business. My professional service must provide a healthy return on investment. To my LGBTI brothers and sisters—my bisexual siblings who are so often invisible and the recipients of suspicion, to my trans family so often the victims of violence or the most aggressive forms of disapproval, to my masculine-identified lesbian sisters who are perceived as a threat to straight men, to my queers brothers who are consistently stripped of their humanity and reduced to sexual behavior, to every contributor to this wonderful collection who bore your soul and relived your trauma to share it as a site of healing—my cry to us as a community is to be sure to get an astonishing return on our investment. And because he, being in the form of God, thought it not robbery to humble himself . . . to the death of the cross . . . God gave him a great name (Phil 2:6–9).

Our promise is that God intends to give queer people of faith a great name. So broaden your vision, expand your horizons, reimagine your options, reach beyond your obvious ability and routine competency. It's our turn to be blessed with an astonishing return on investment. Don't just live but expect to thrive. Be the church and anticipate the results of loving the church.

Our Witness is more than necessary and timely, it's a contribution to the church's next testament.

Bishop Joseph Tolton is the Bishop of Global Ministries for the Fellowship of Affirming Ministries (TFAM). Bishop Tolton's ministry provides leadership to TFAM's justice collaborations and ministry affiliations outside of the United States. In this capacity, Tolton provides pastoral care and institutional mentorship for LGBTIQ communities in Uganda, Rwanda, Kenya, Cote d'Ivoire, and the DRC. Additionally, Bishop Tolton partners with local clergy and denominations in each of these countries to pioneer a pan-African open and affirming progressive Christian movement. After graduating from Vassar College in 1989 with a BA in Religion, Tolton also earned an MBA from the Columbia Business School.